Thomas Rowlandson

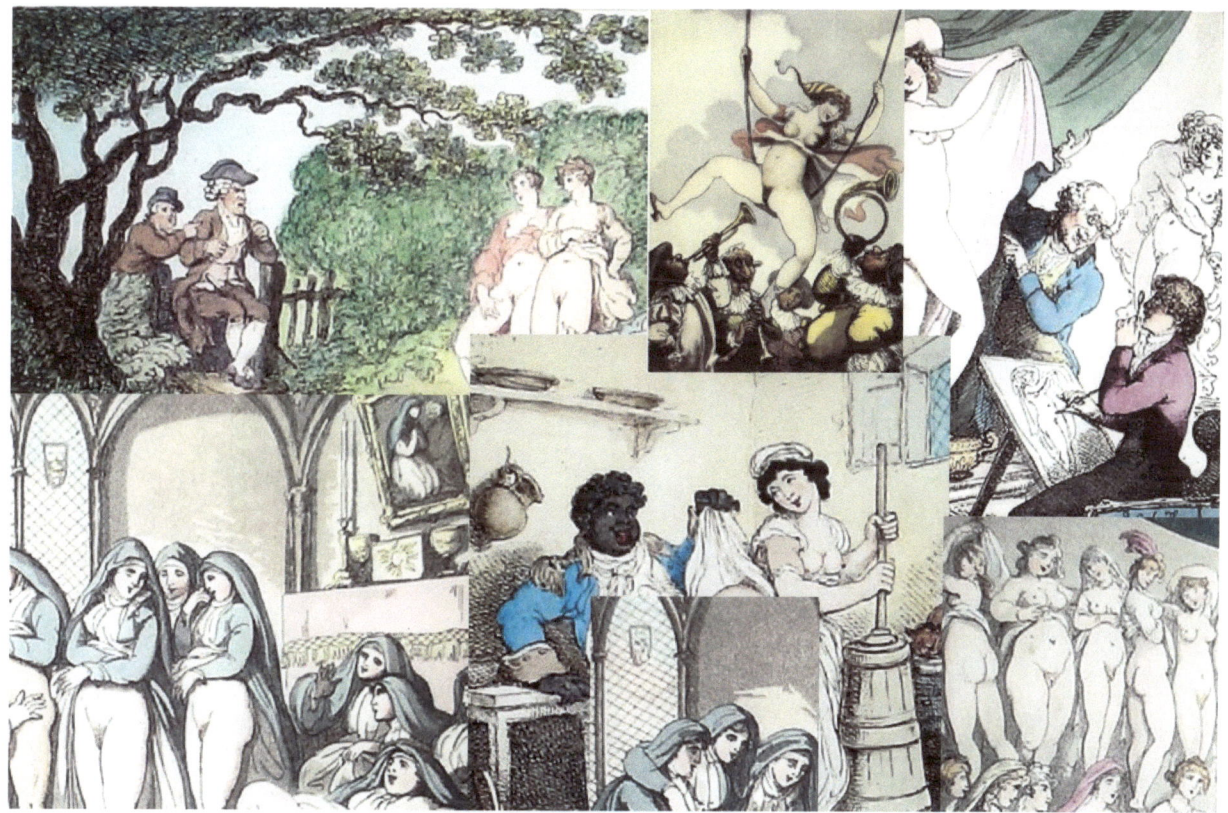

Edited By Lacey Belinda Smith

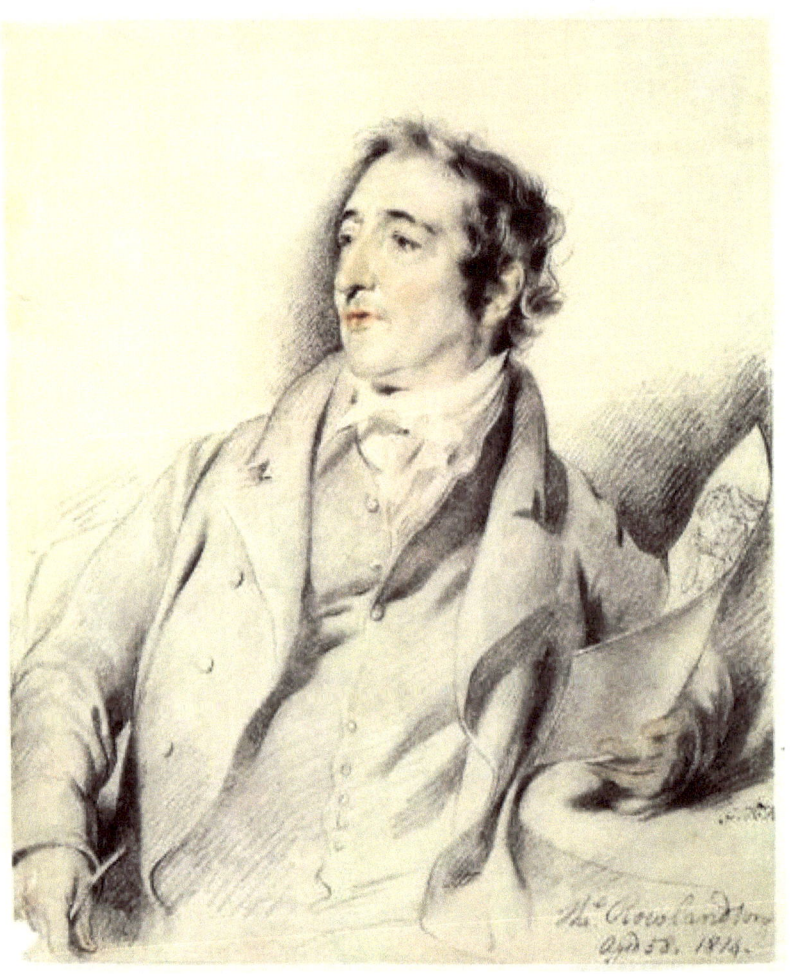

Thomas Rowlandson (1756 – 1827) was an English artist and caricaturist.

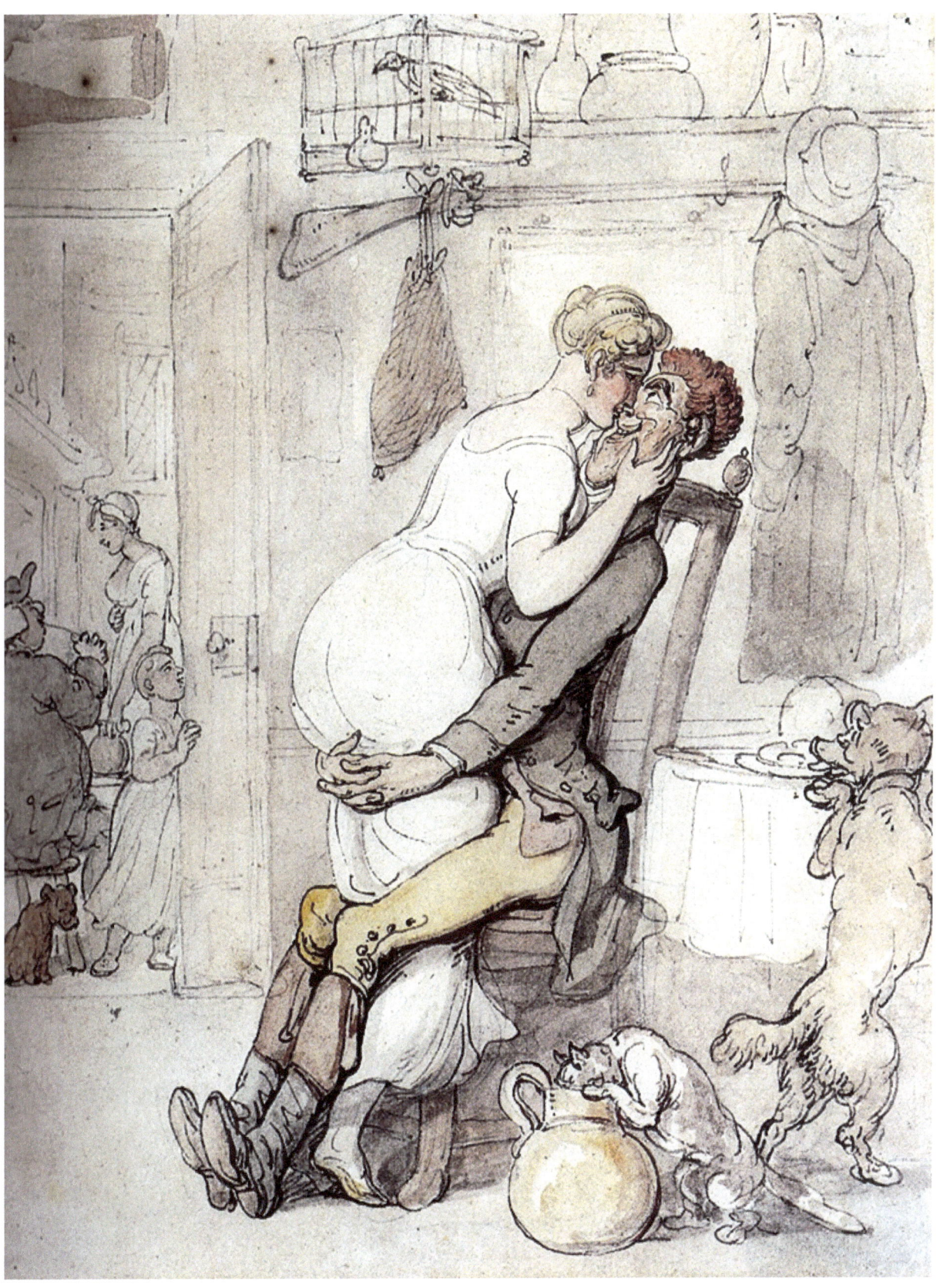

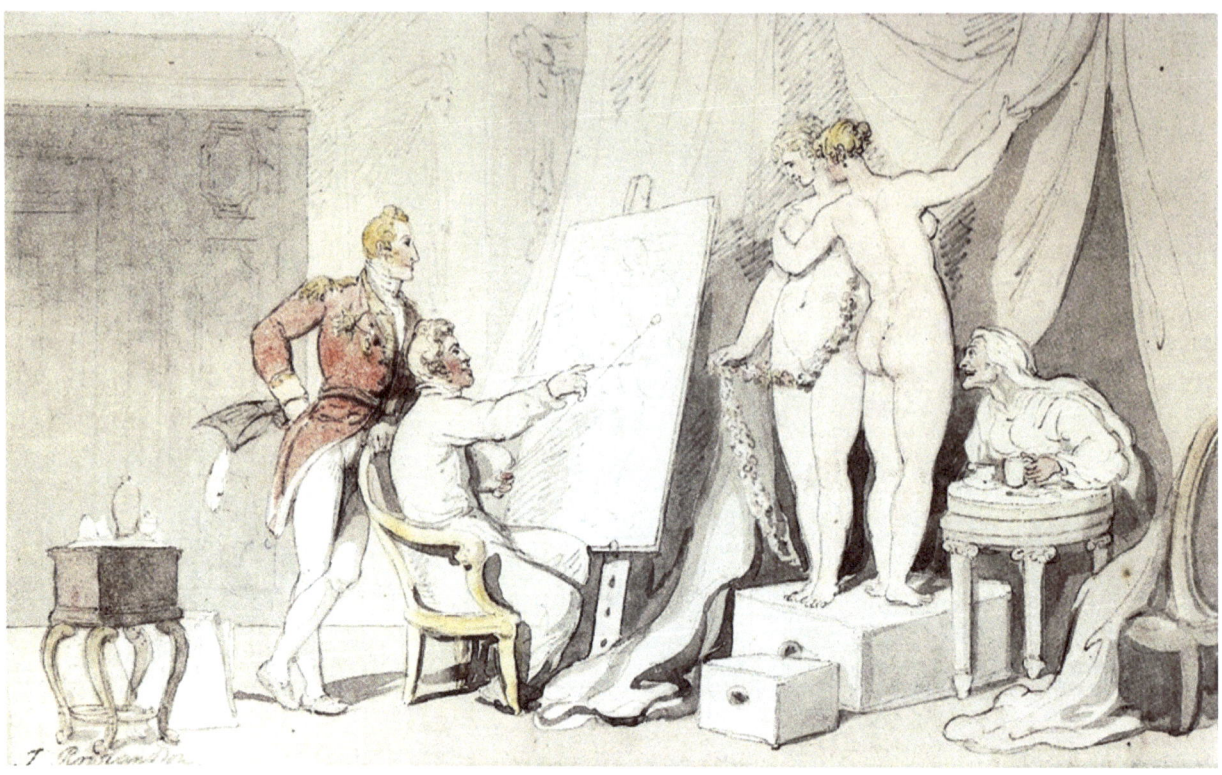

Thomas Rowlandson

Thomas Rowlandson was one of the leading caricaturists of Georgian England. He was the son of a successful businessman. The absurdities of fashion, the perils of love, political and royal intrigue, drawings of popular and low-life subjects were the daily subject matter of Thomas Rowlandson-- life at the turn of the 19th century. Rowlandson was working at a time when English satirical prints were prized by collectors across Europe. A number of the works in the exhibitions were purchased by George, Prince of Wales, later Prince Regent and King George IV. Incongruently, the Prince was often the butt of caricaturists' jokes and, as a result, sometimes tried to prevent the publication of images that he felt were particularly opprobrious.

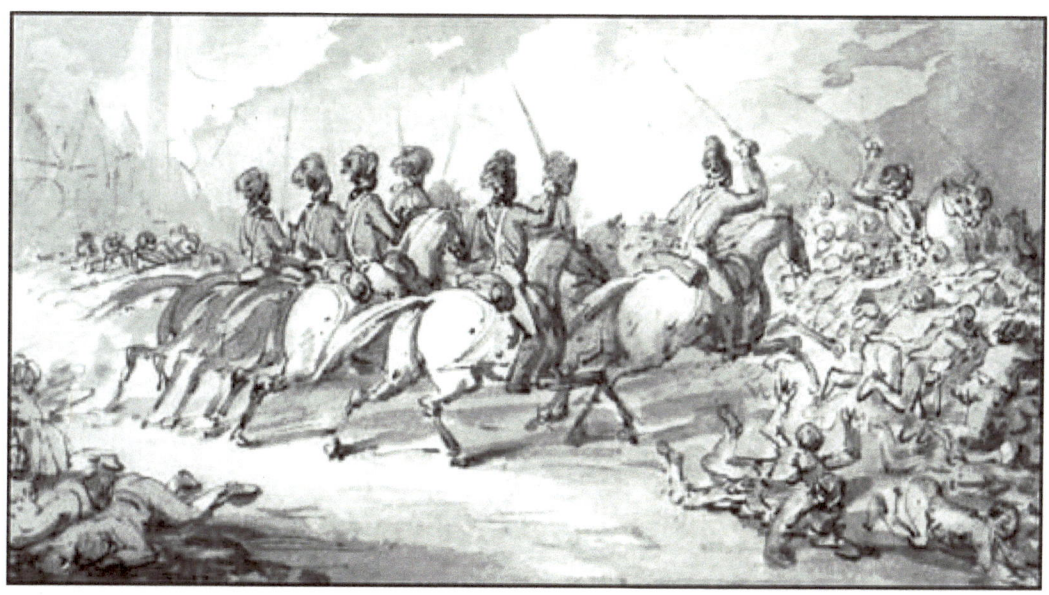

Thomas Rowlandson, *Mounted Cavalry Charging a Crowd* (1819) Peterloo Massacre

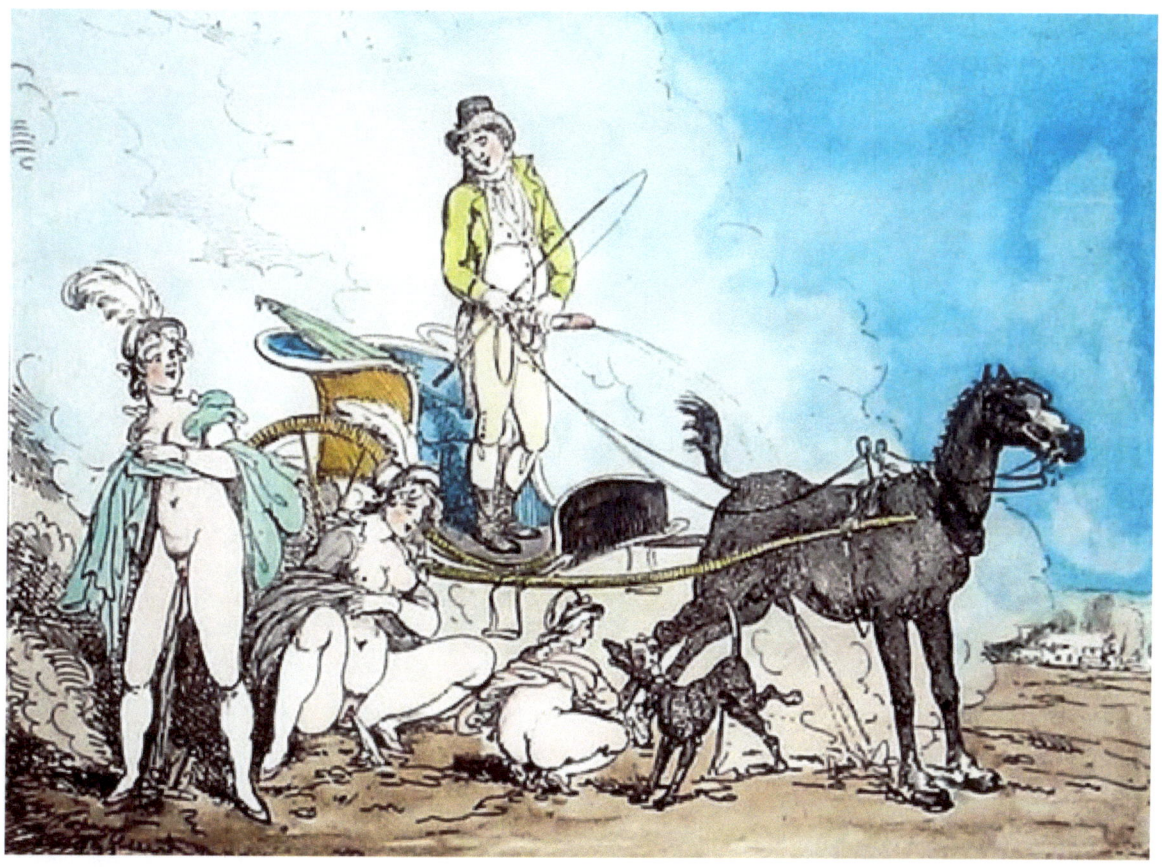

A Family on a Journey laying the Dust

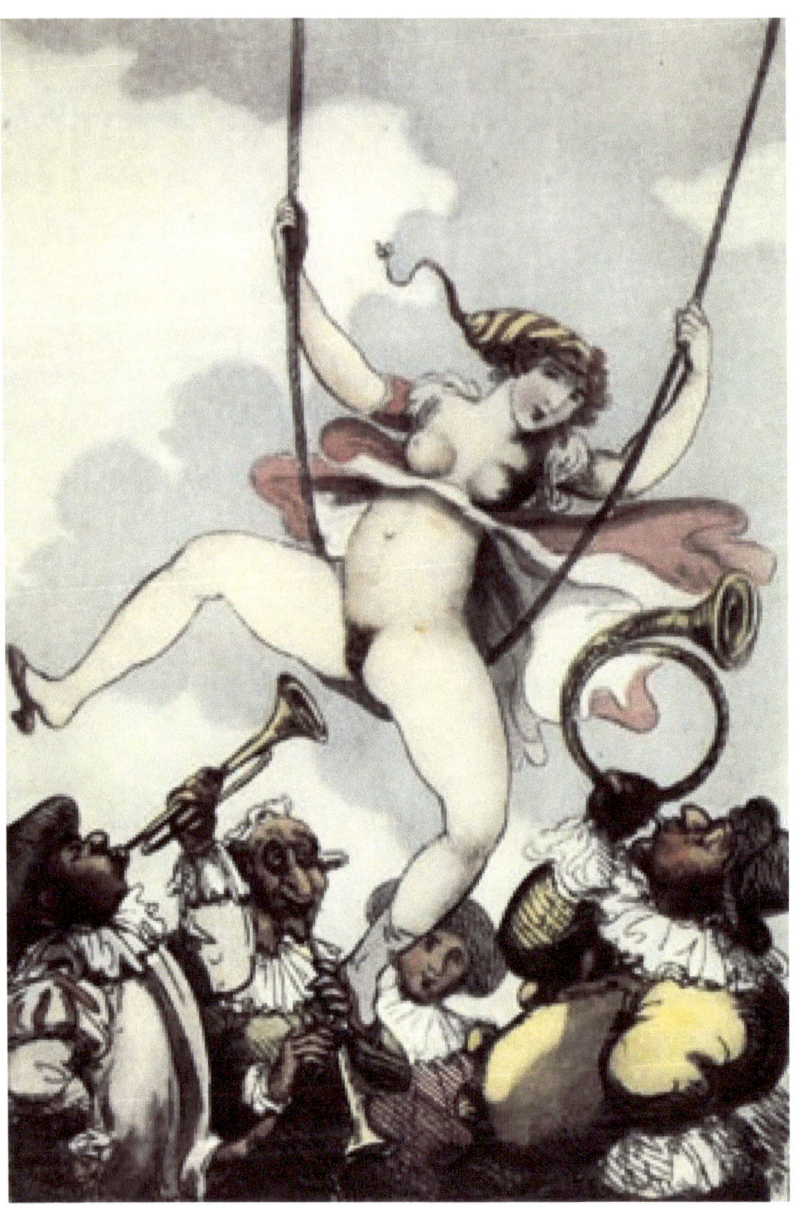

The Swing

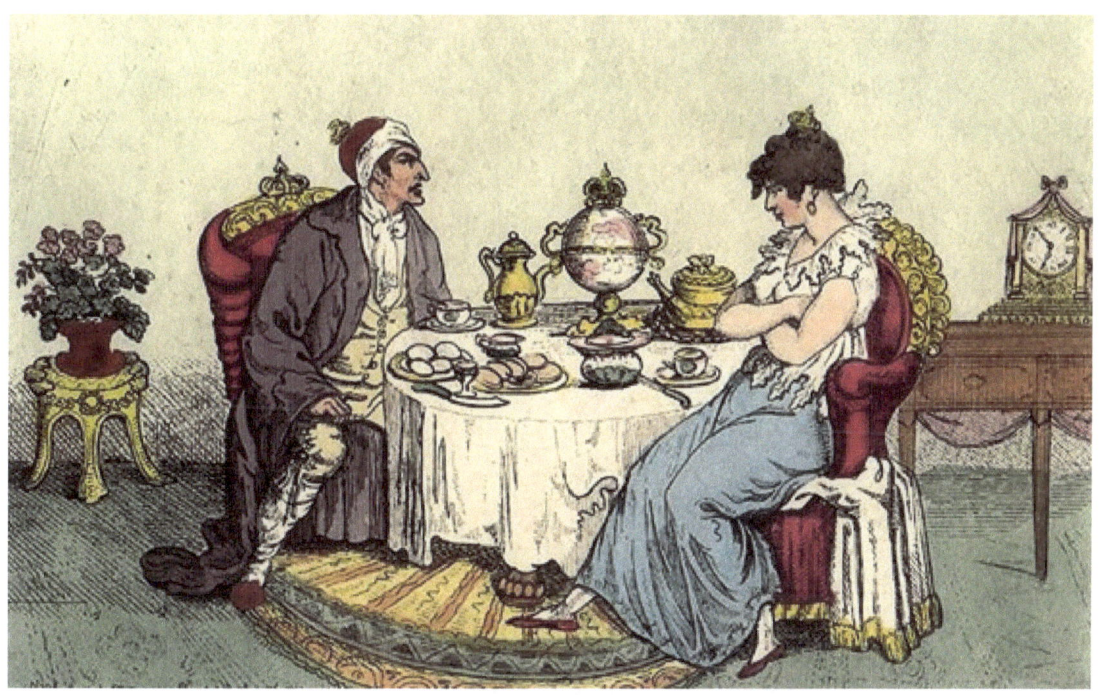

"Boney and his New Wife, or a Quarrell about Nothing"

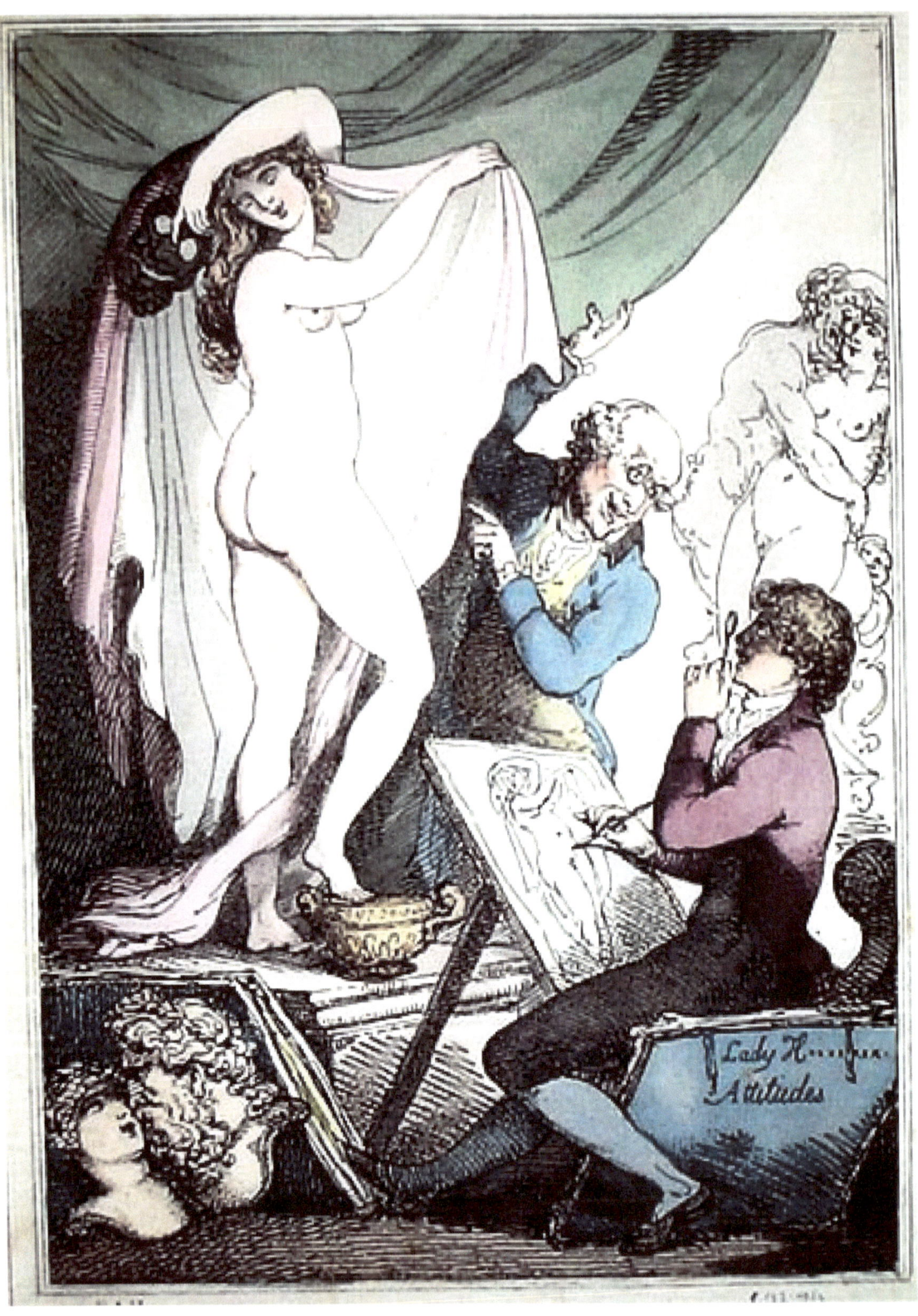

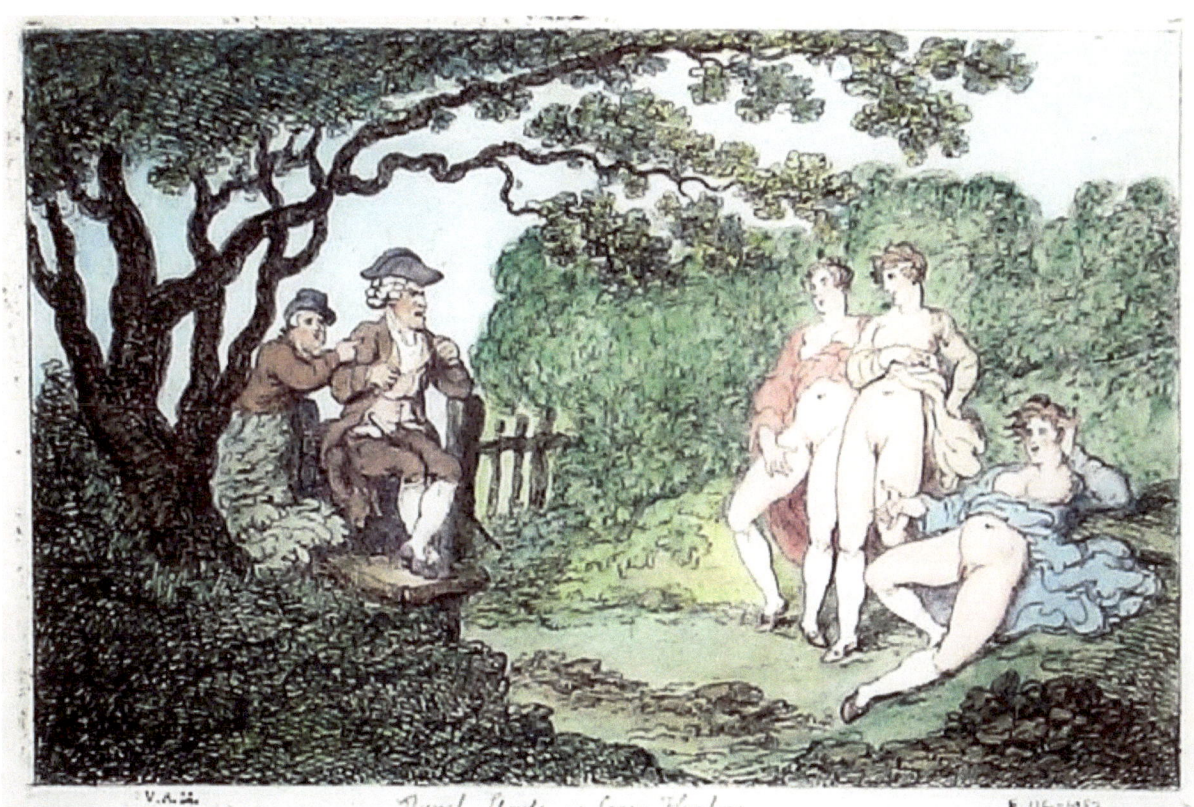

Rural Sports or Coney Hunting

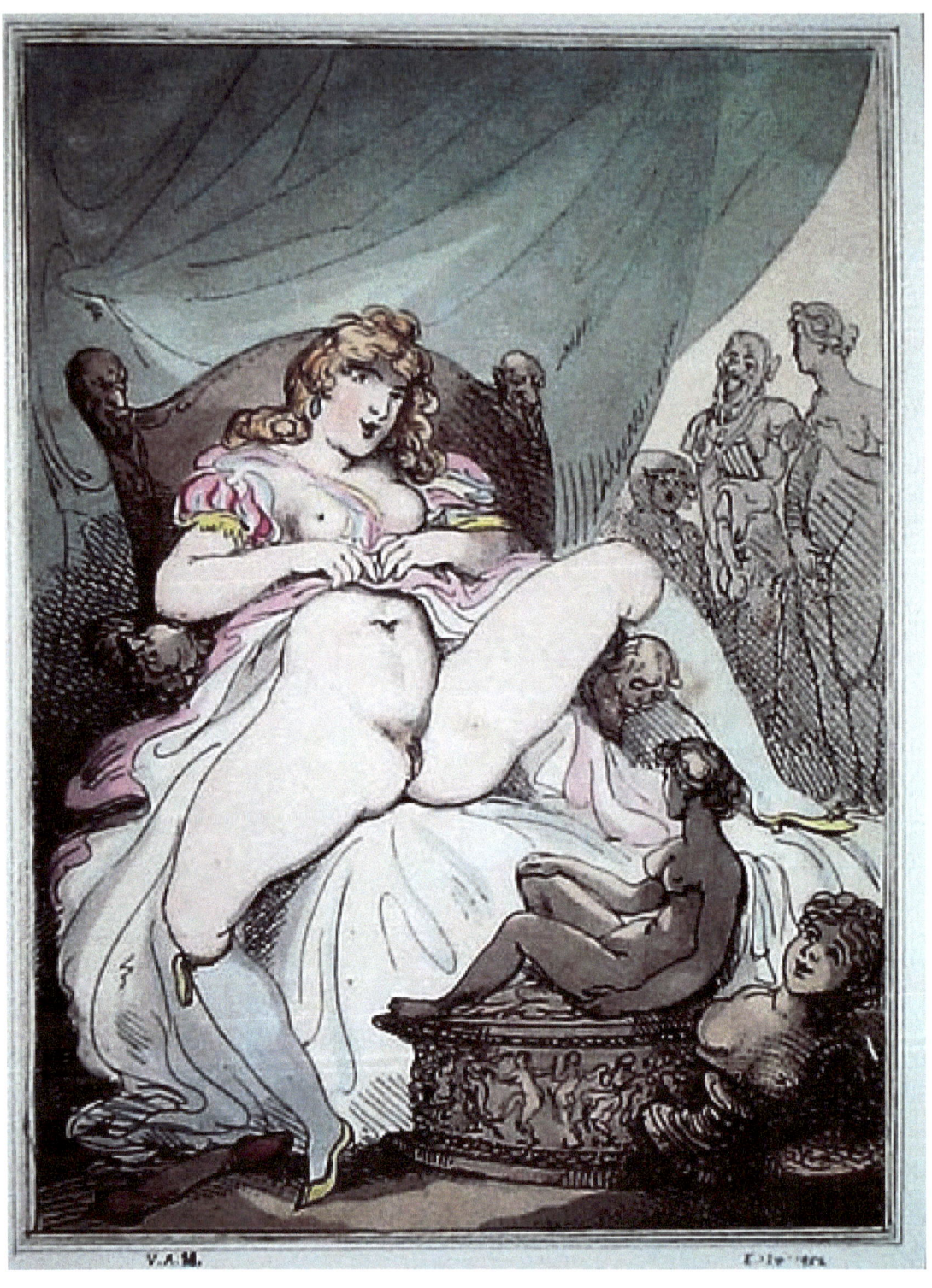

Solitary diversion

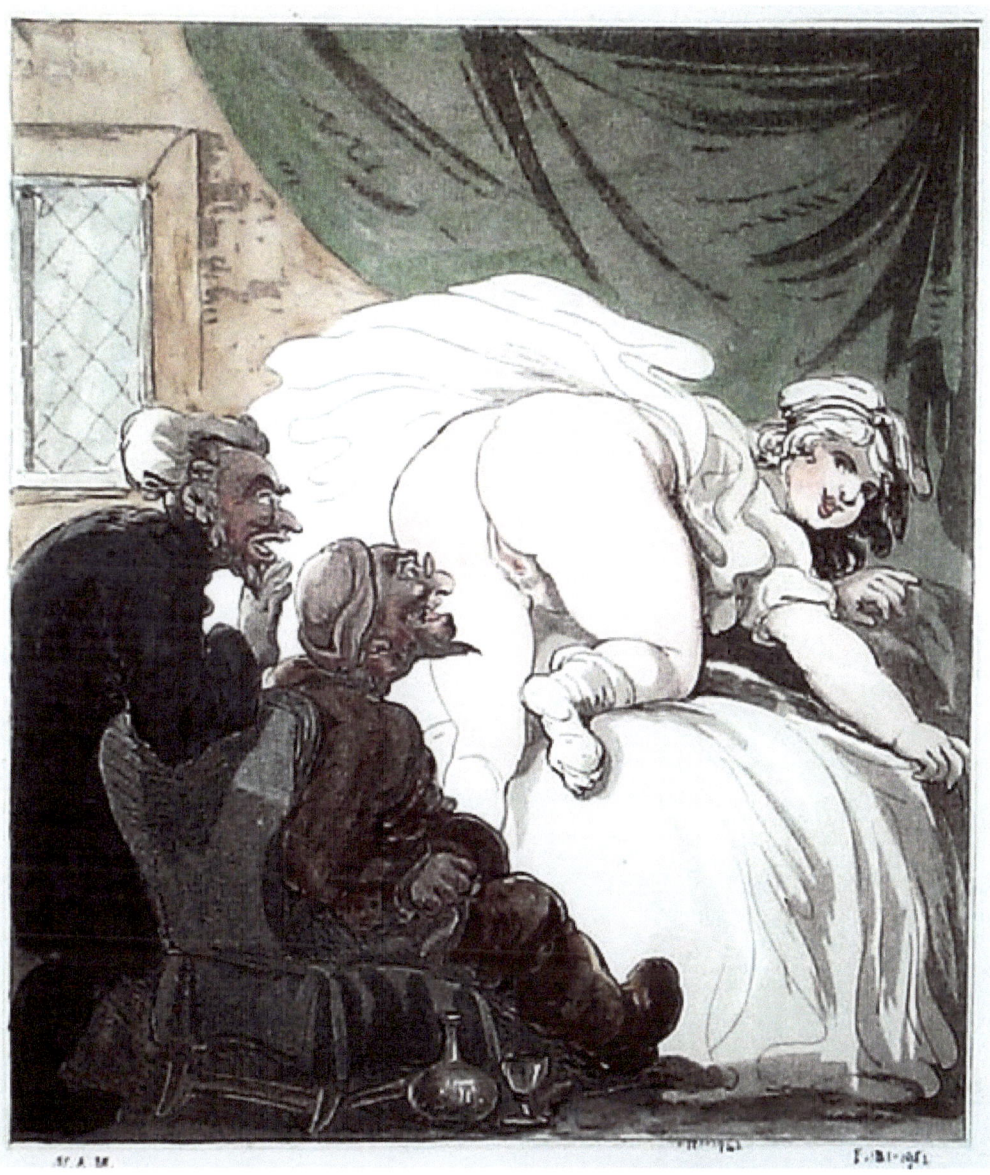

Susanna and the Elders

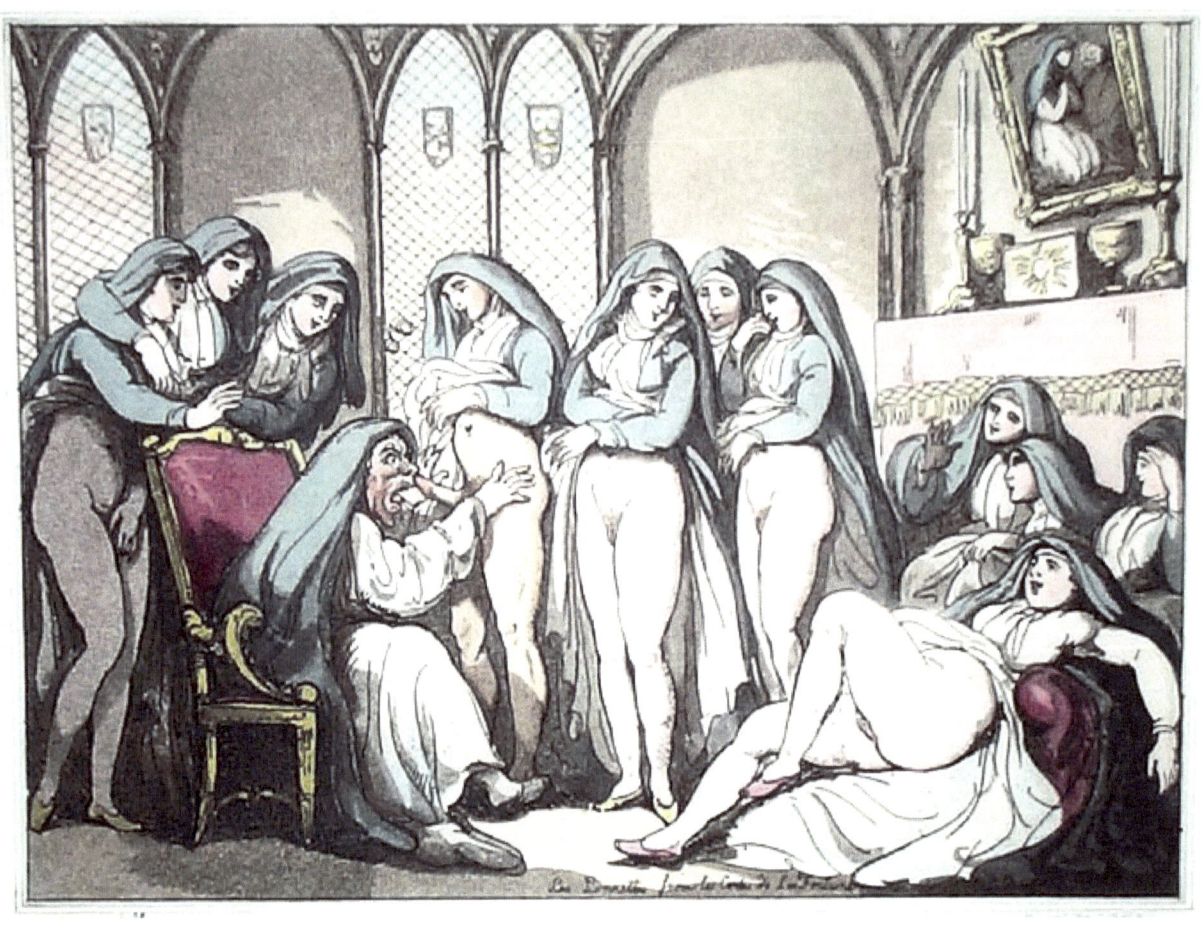

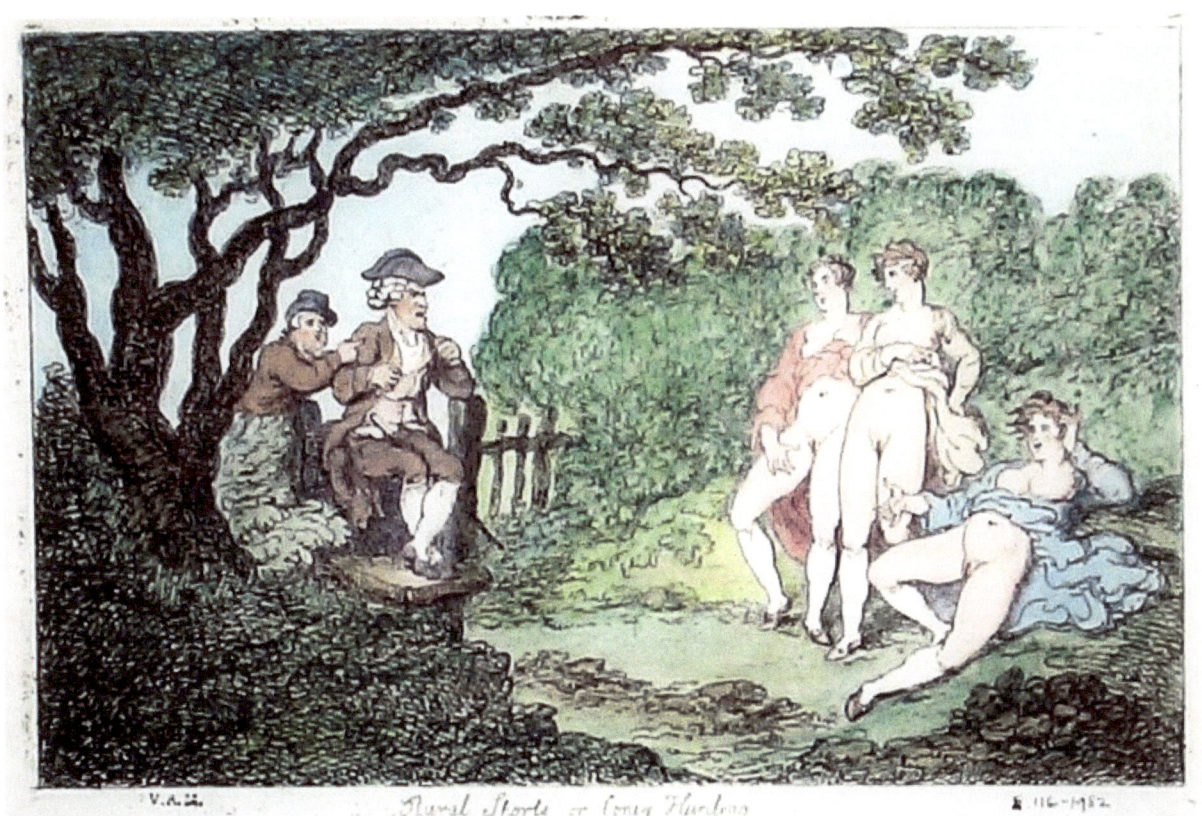

V.A.2.   Rural Sports or Coney Hunting   E 116-1982

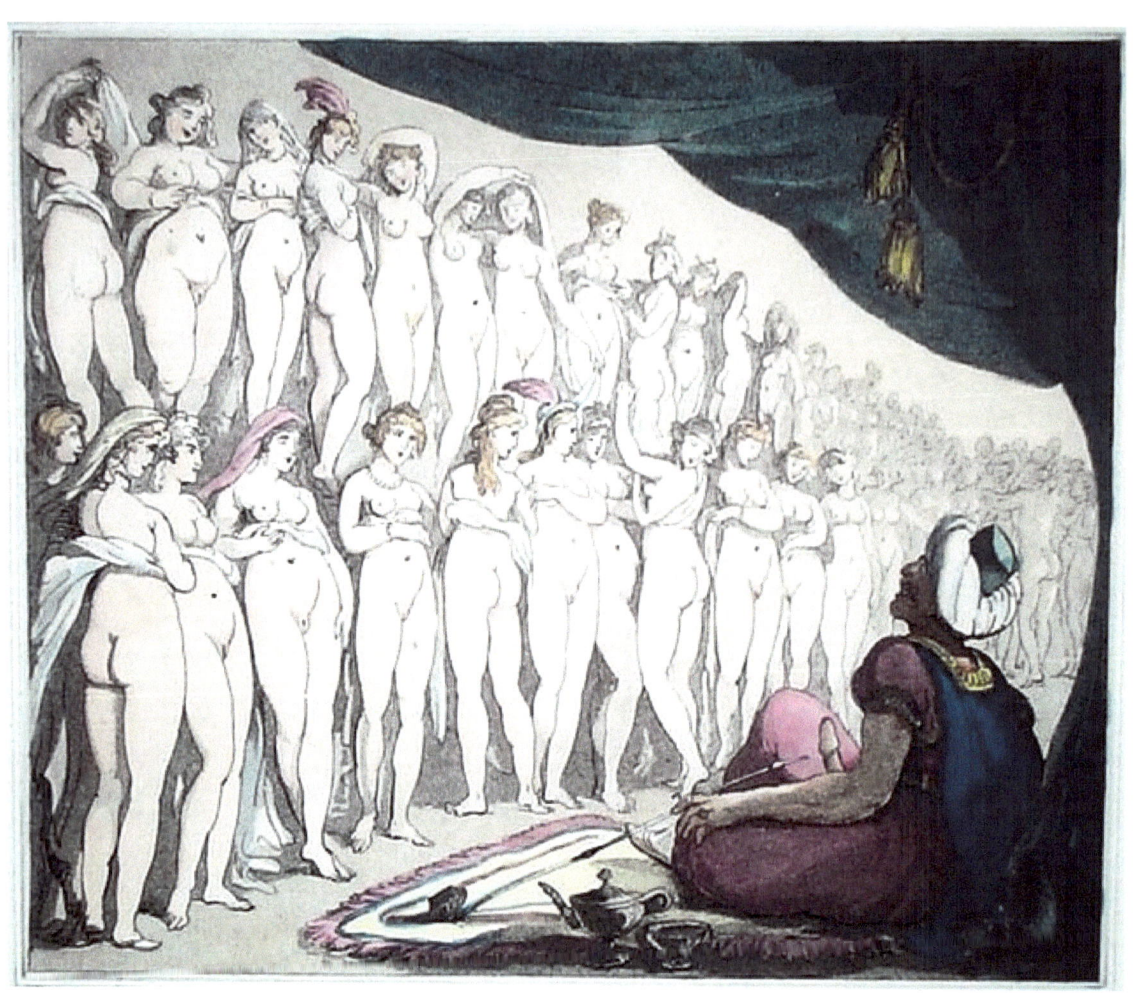

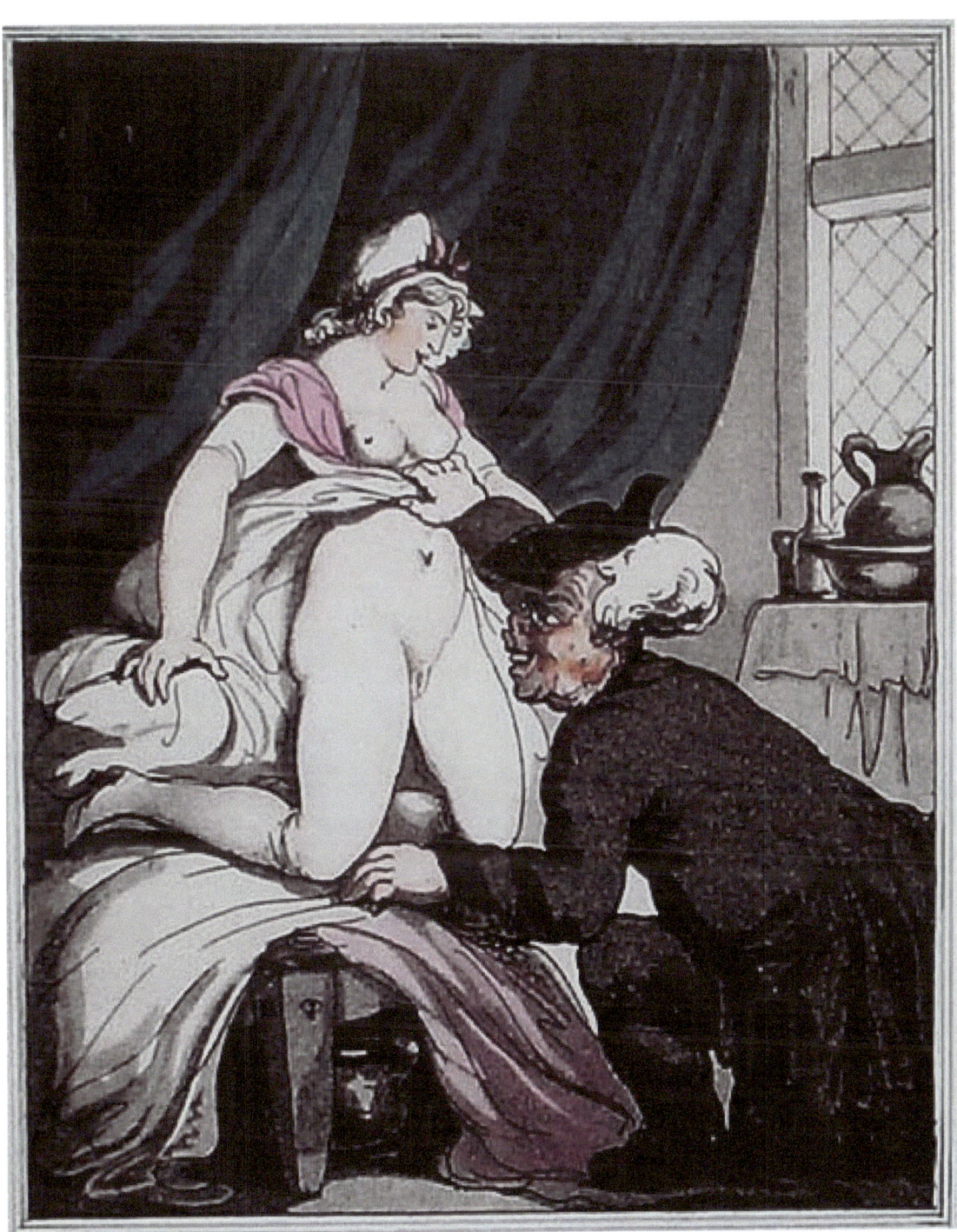

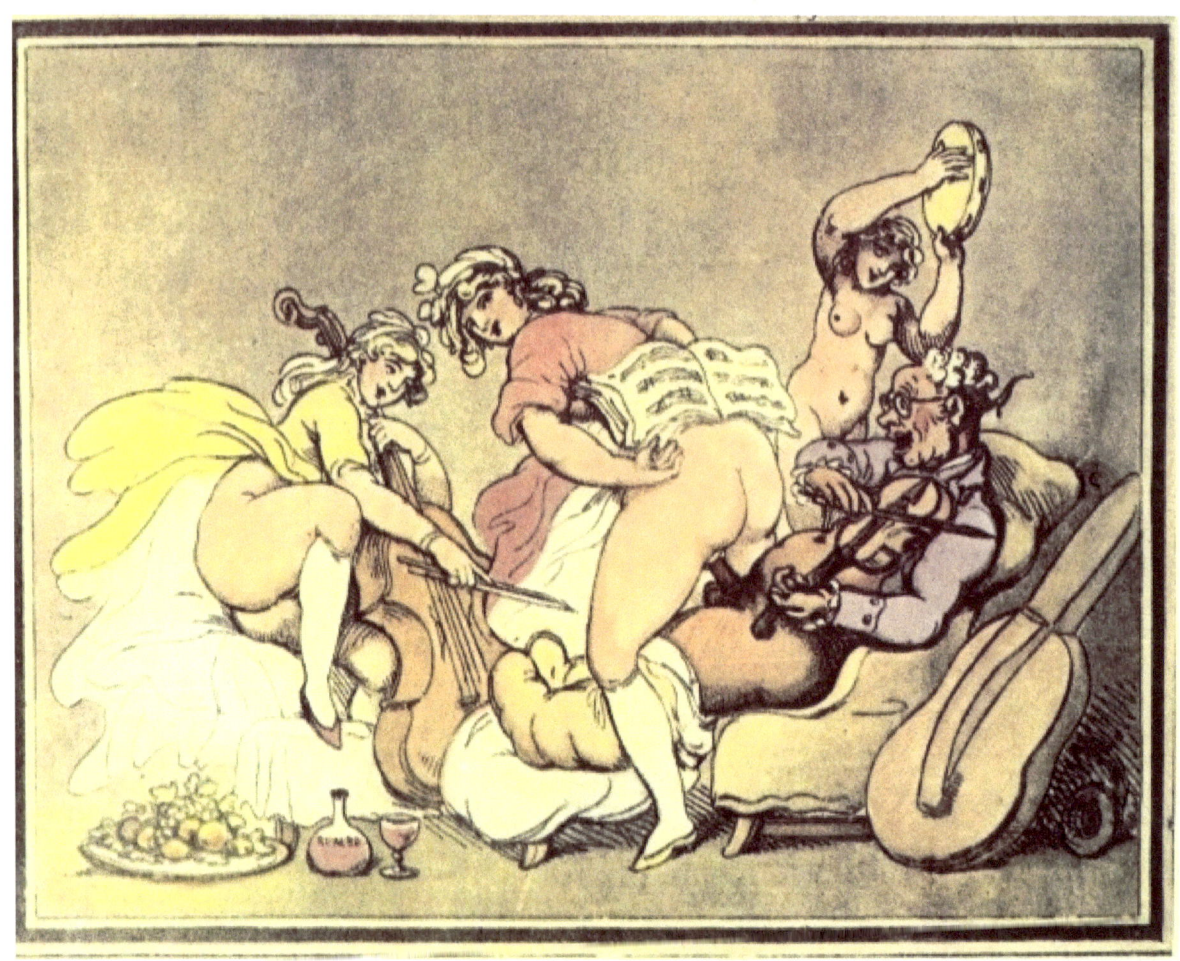

The Concert

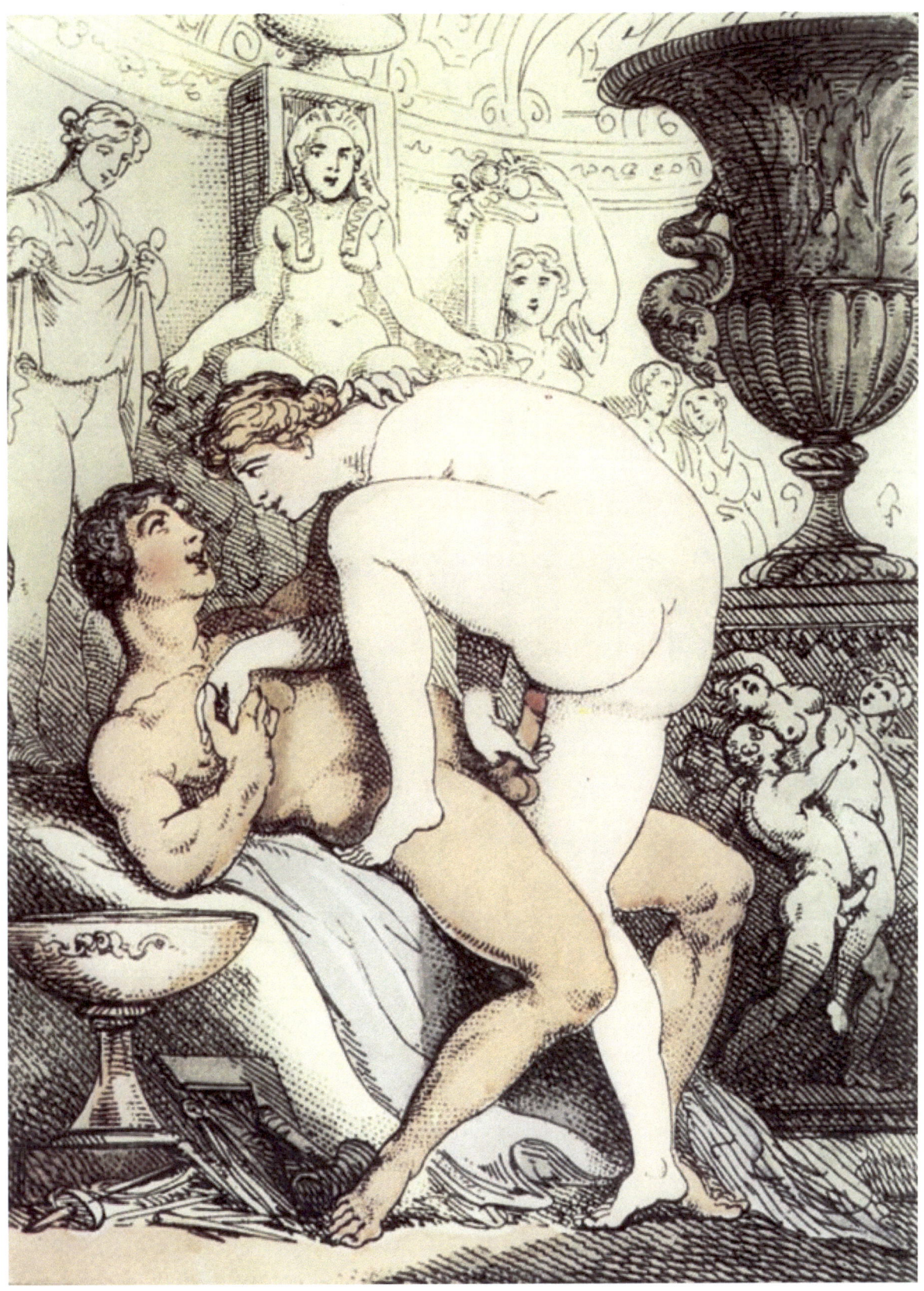

Modern Pygmalion

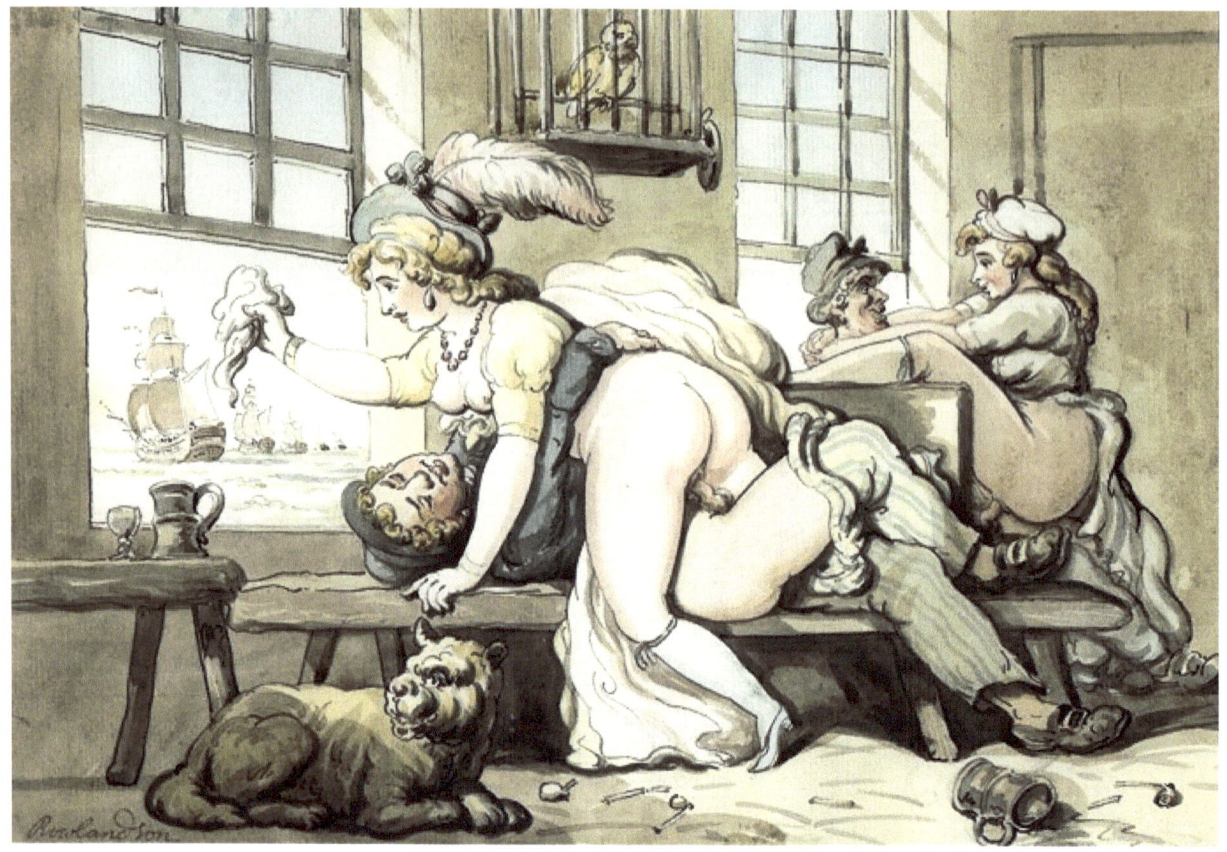

Goodbye

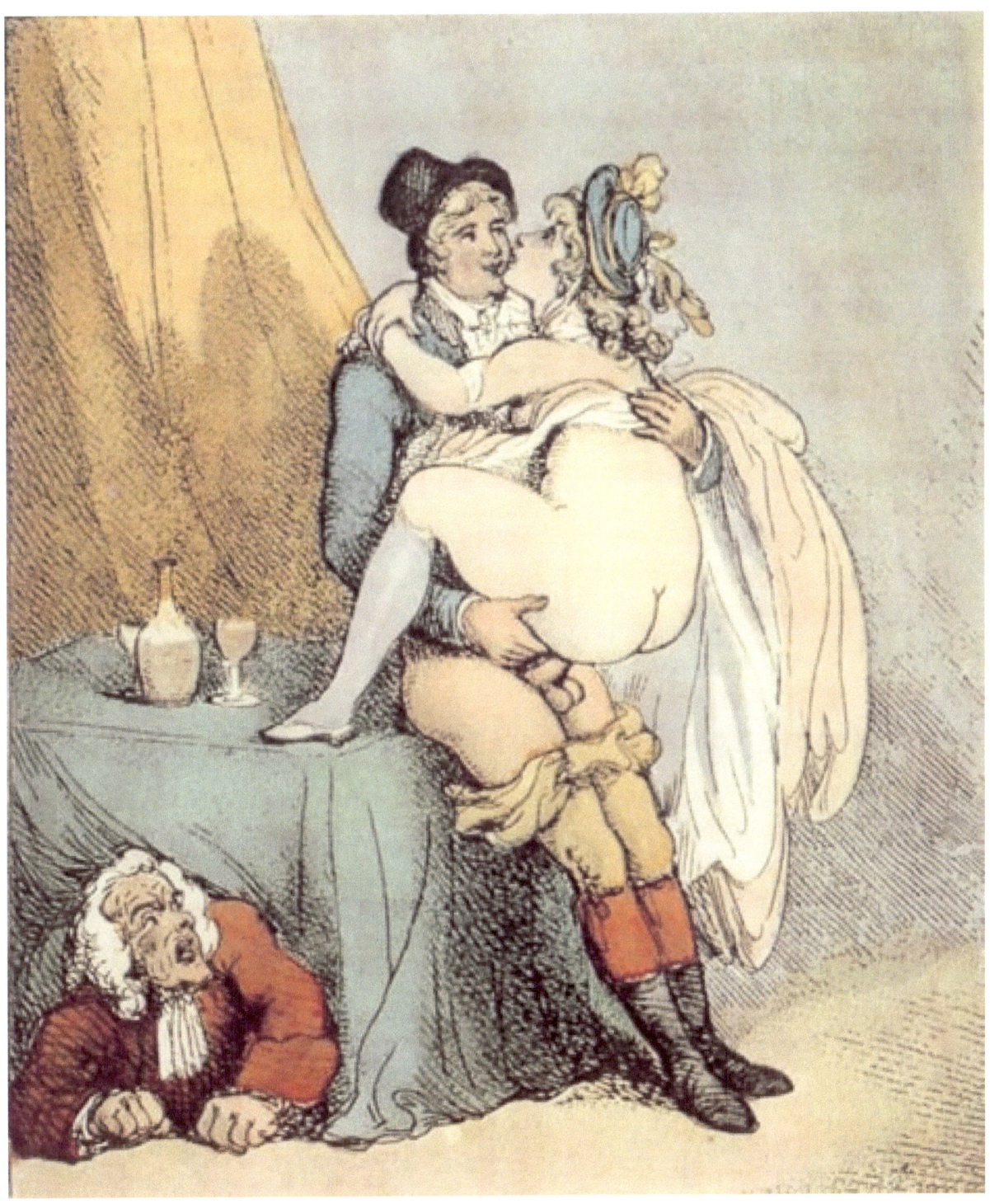

The Rightful Lover comes out of the Wings.

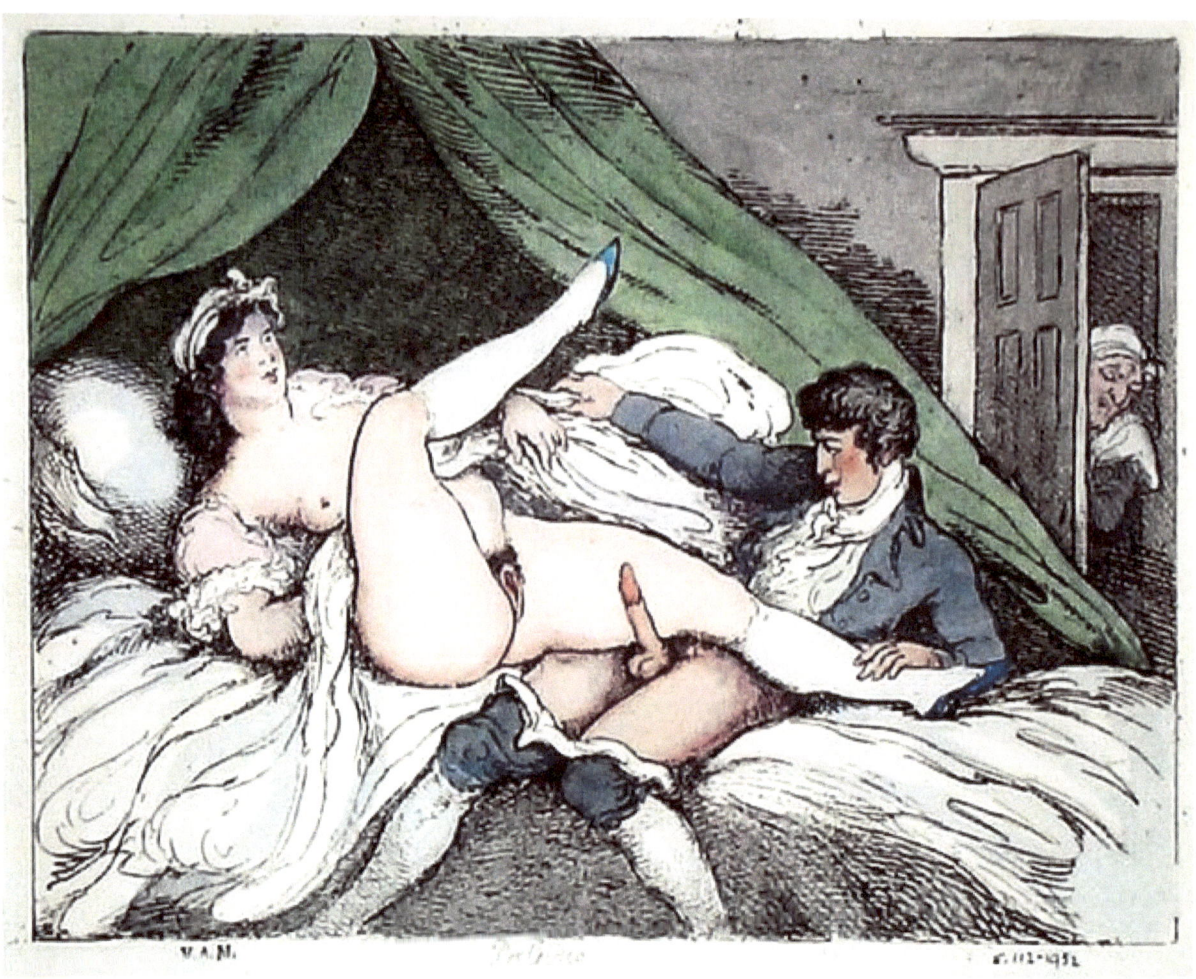

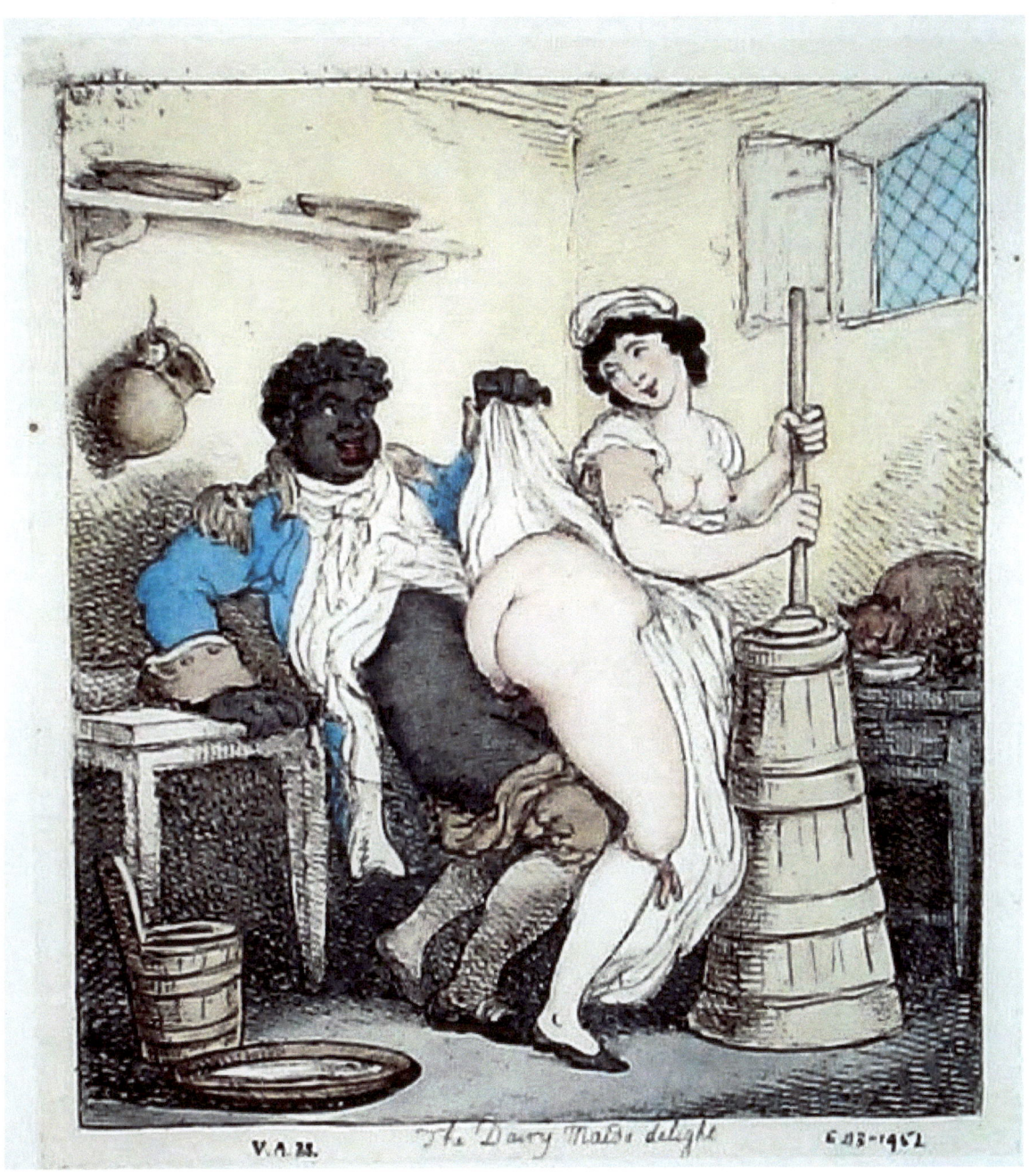

The Dairy Maid's delight

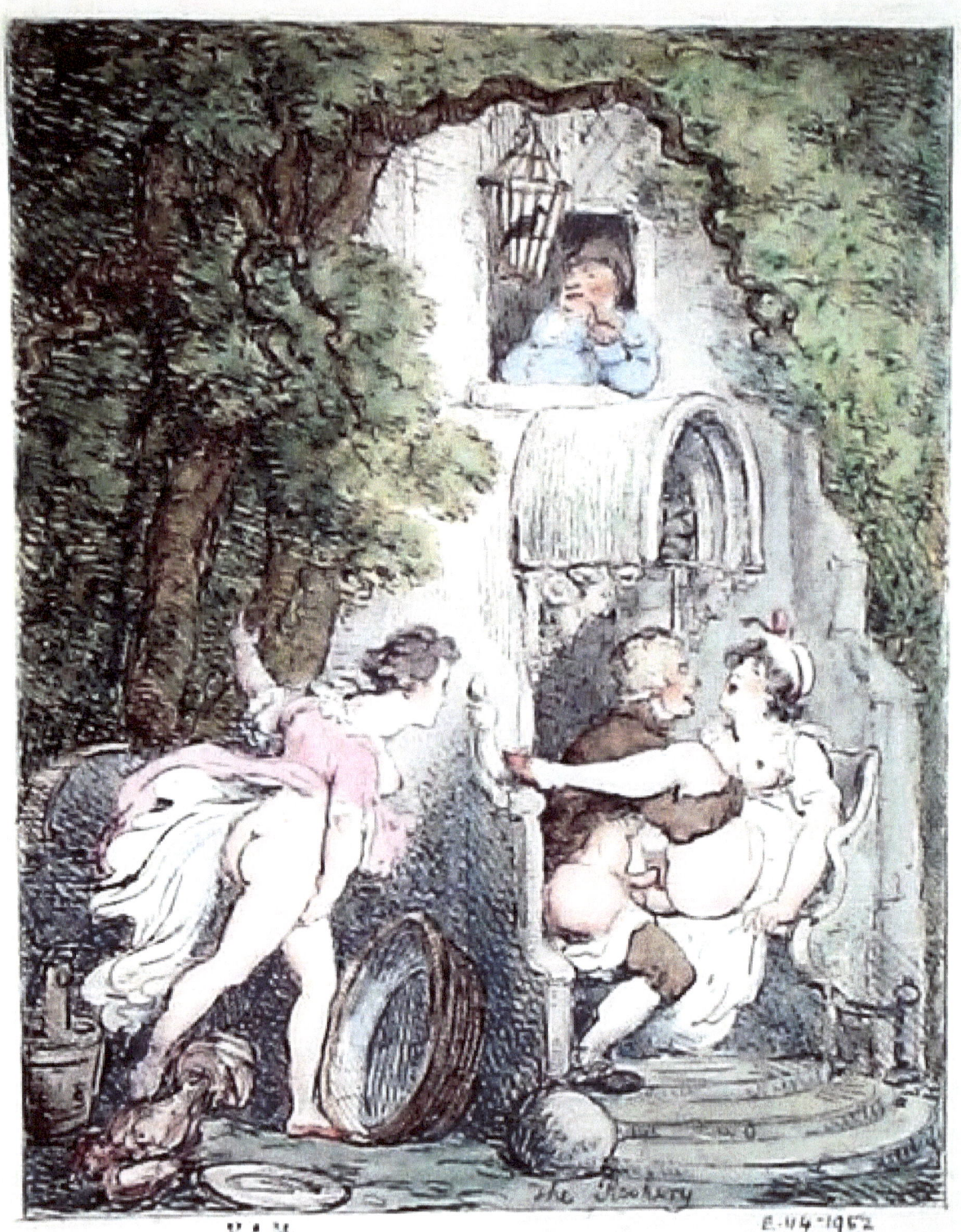

The Rookery

V.A.M.   E.44-1952

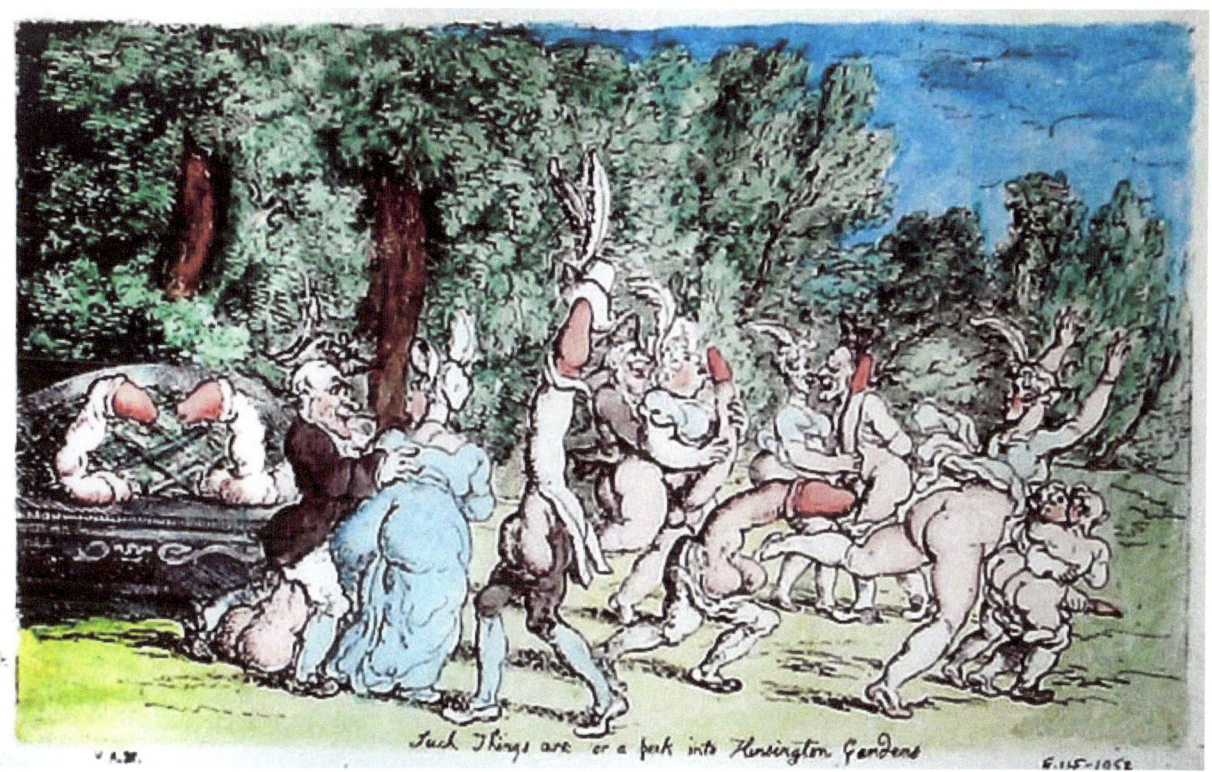

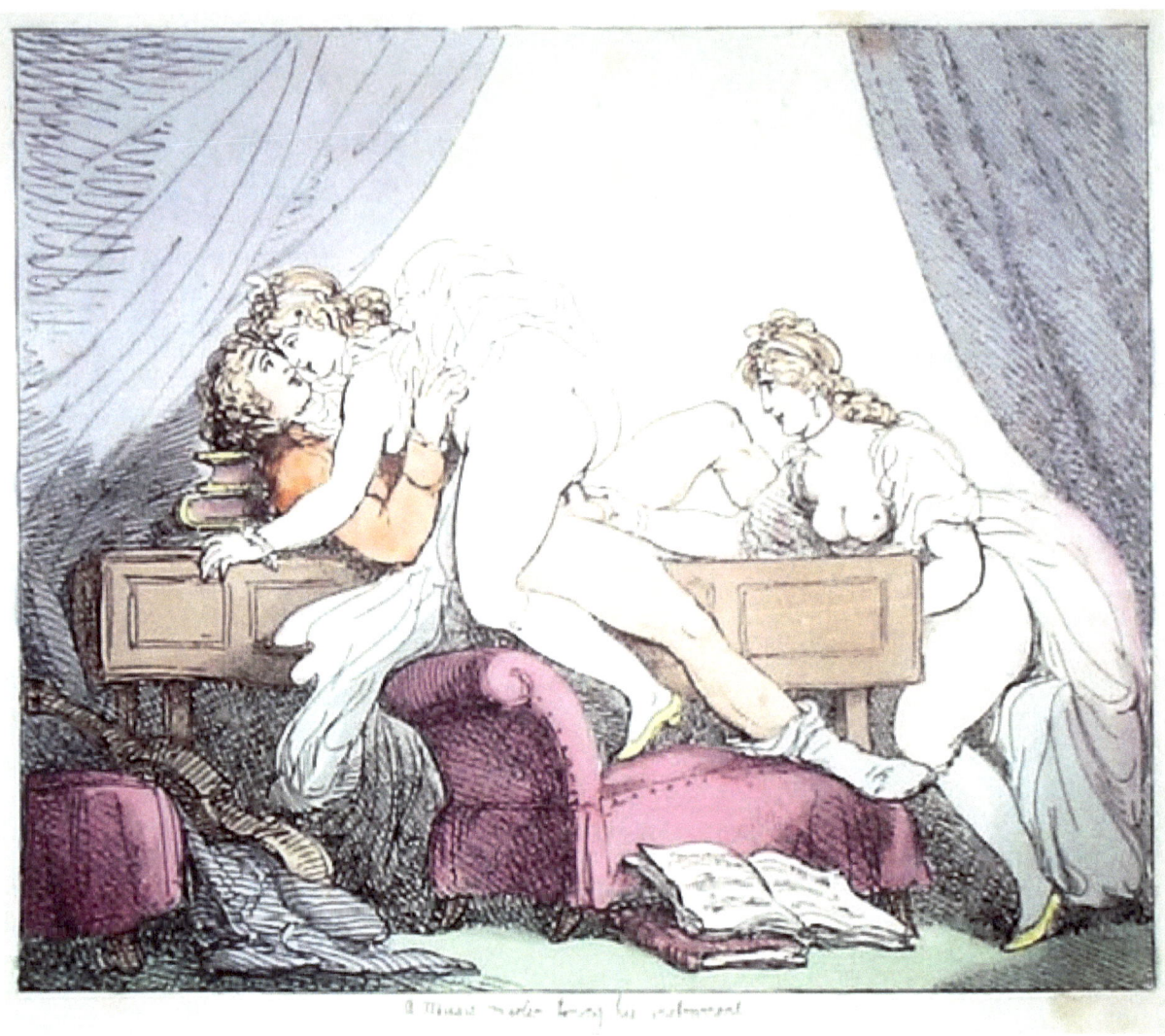

A Muse madam being his informant

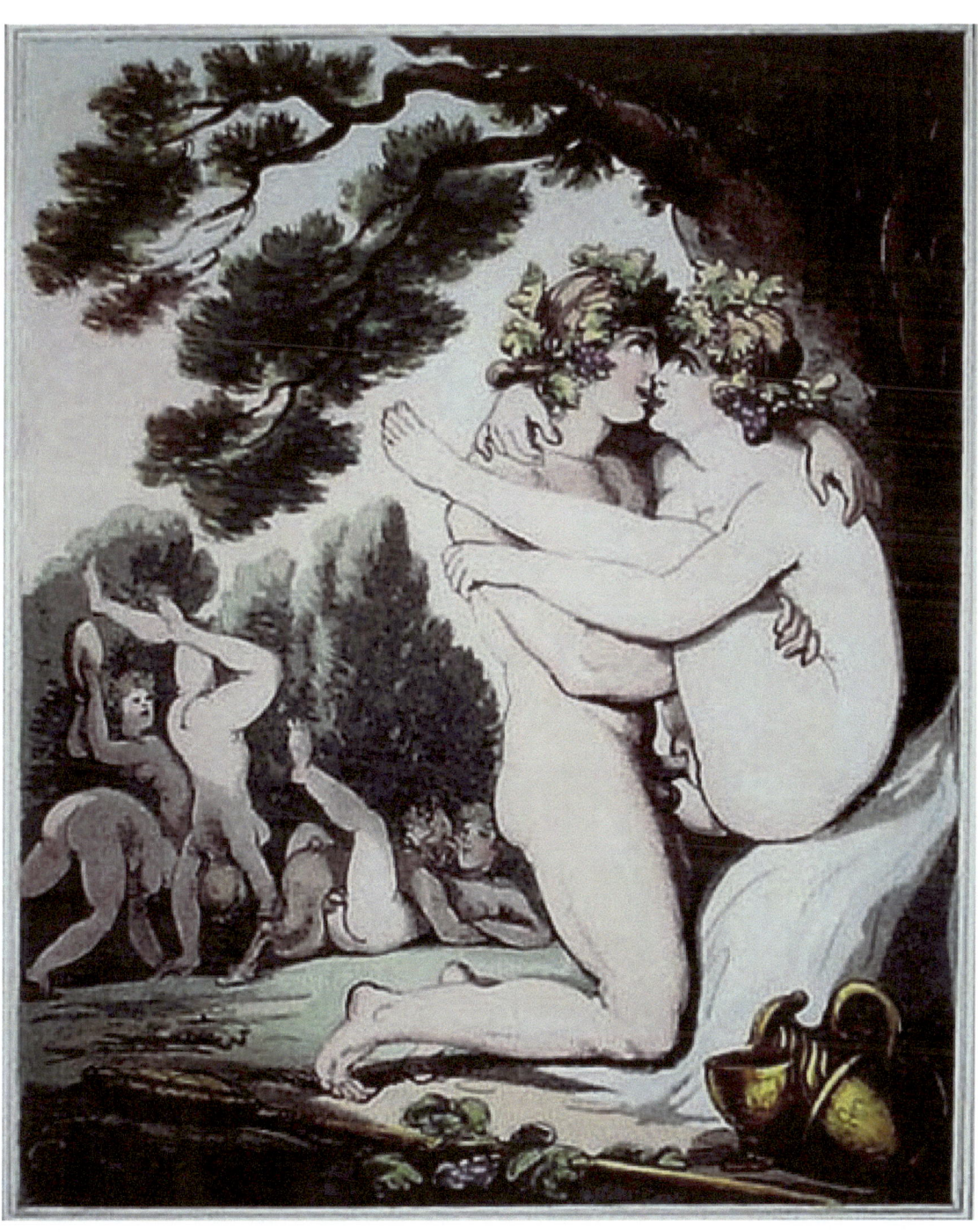

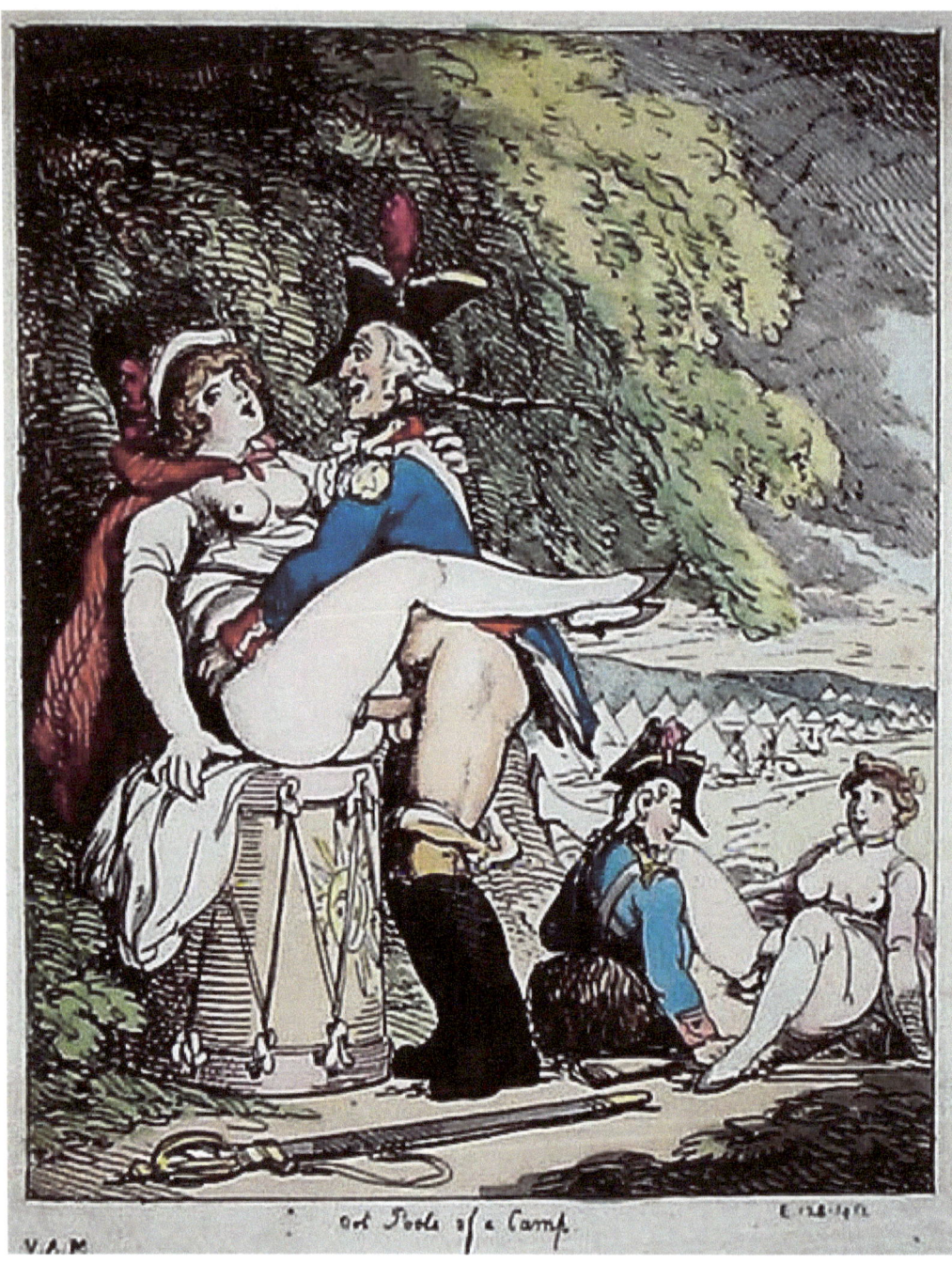

On the Battlefield

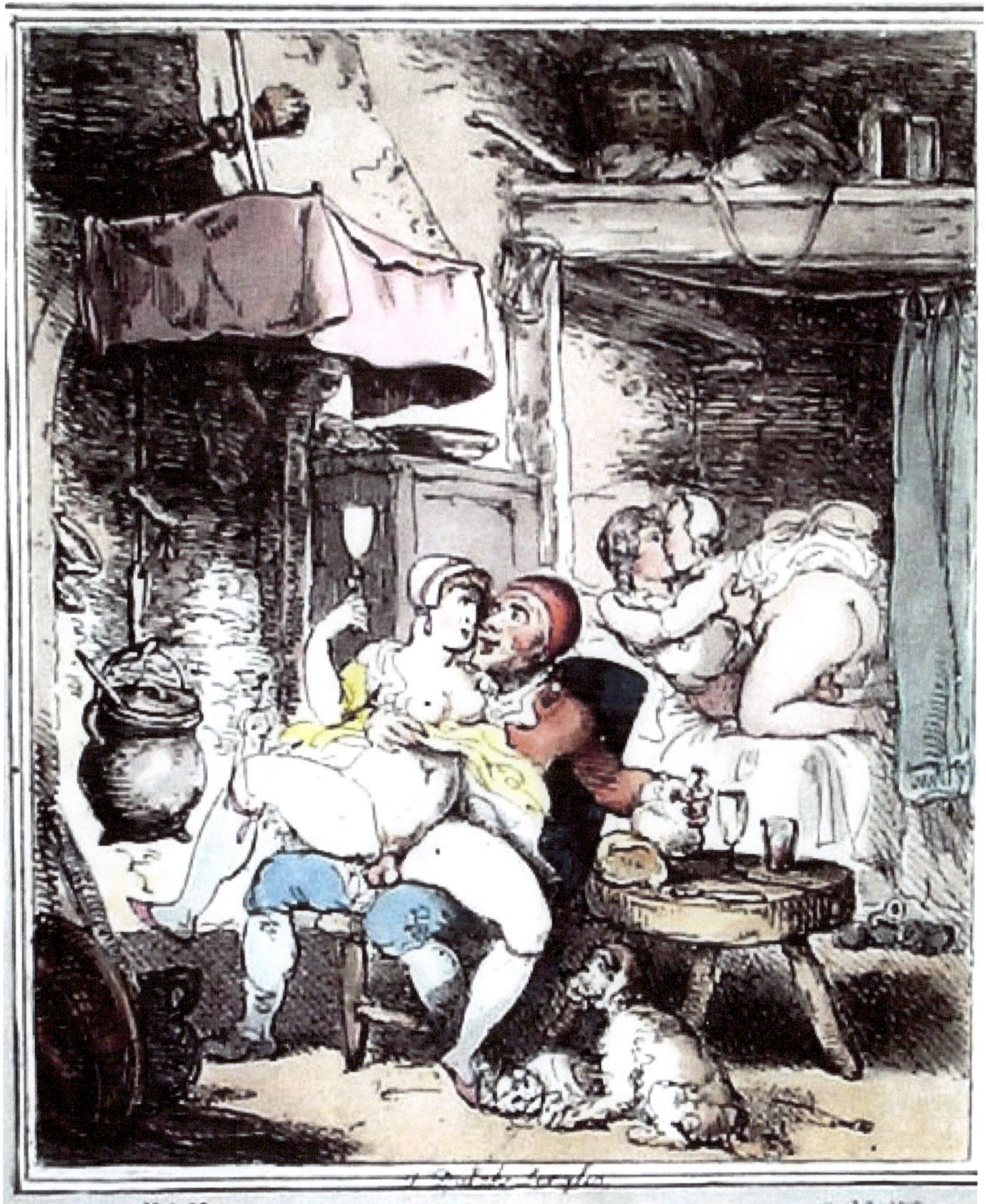

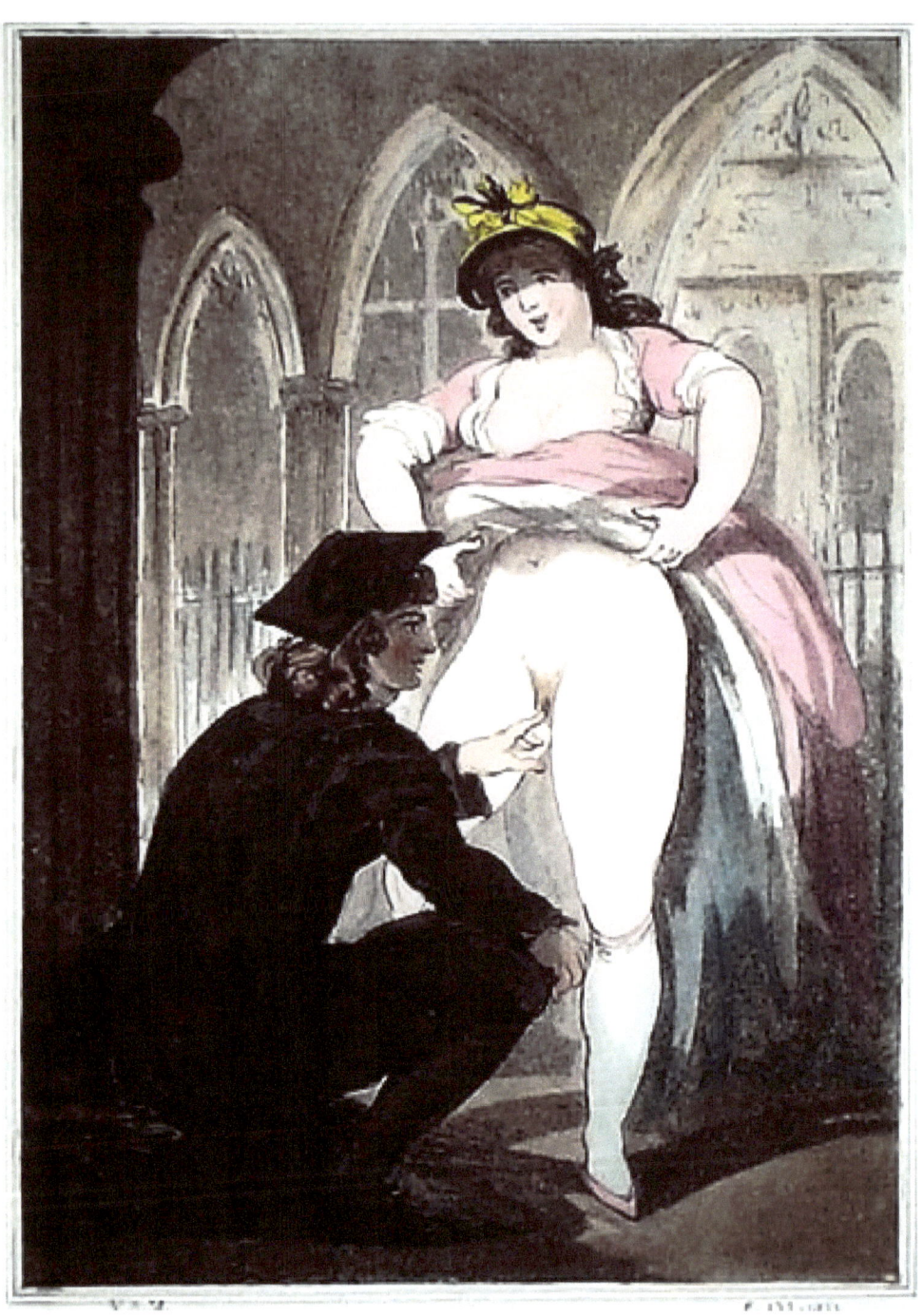

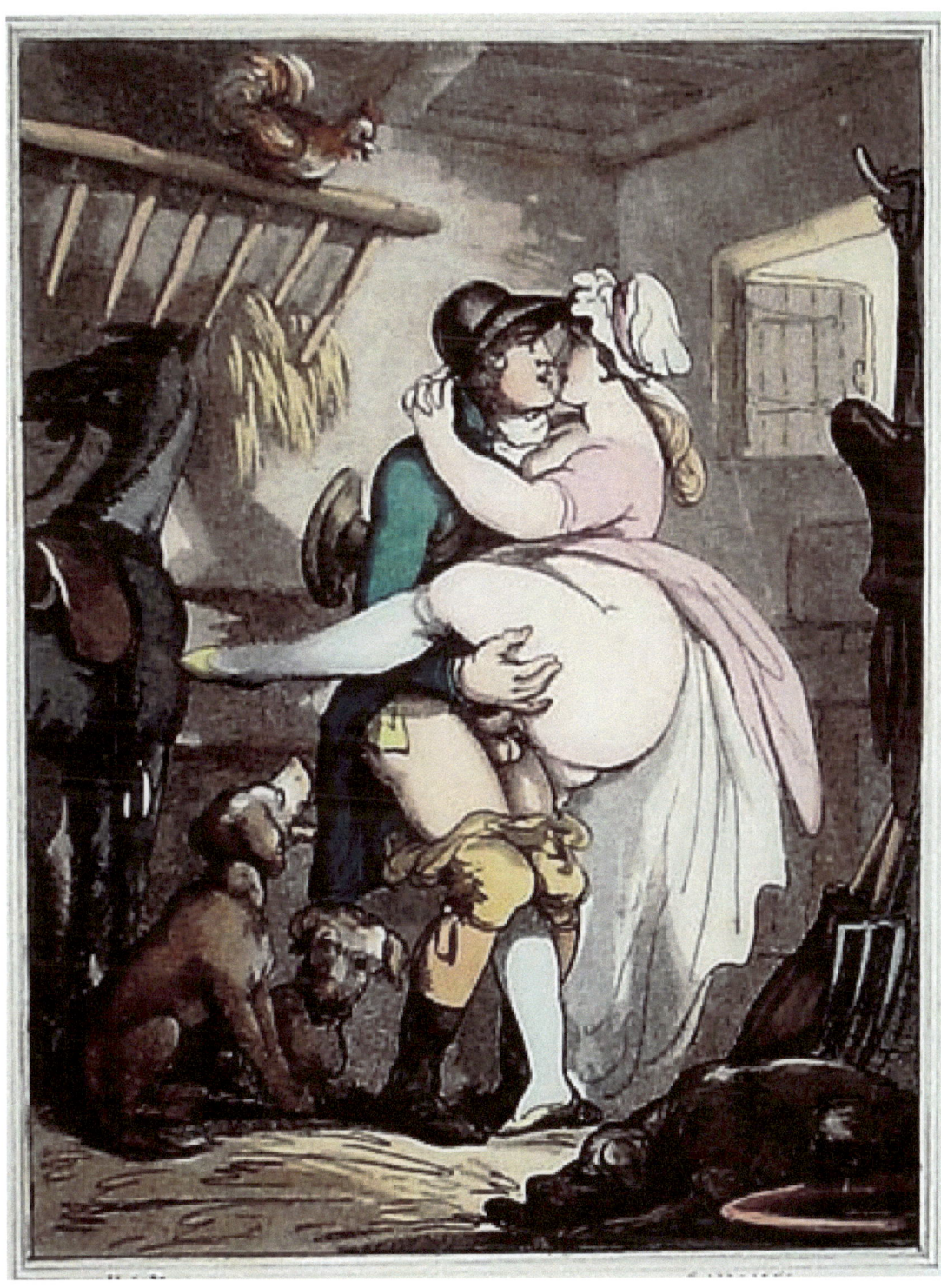

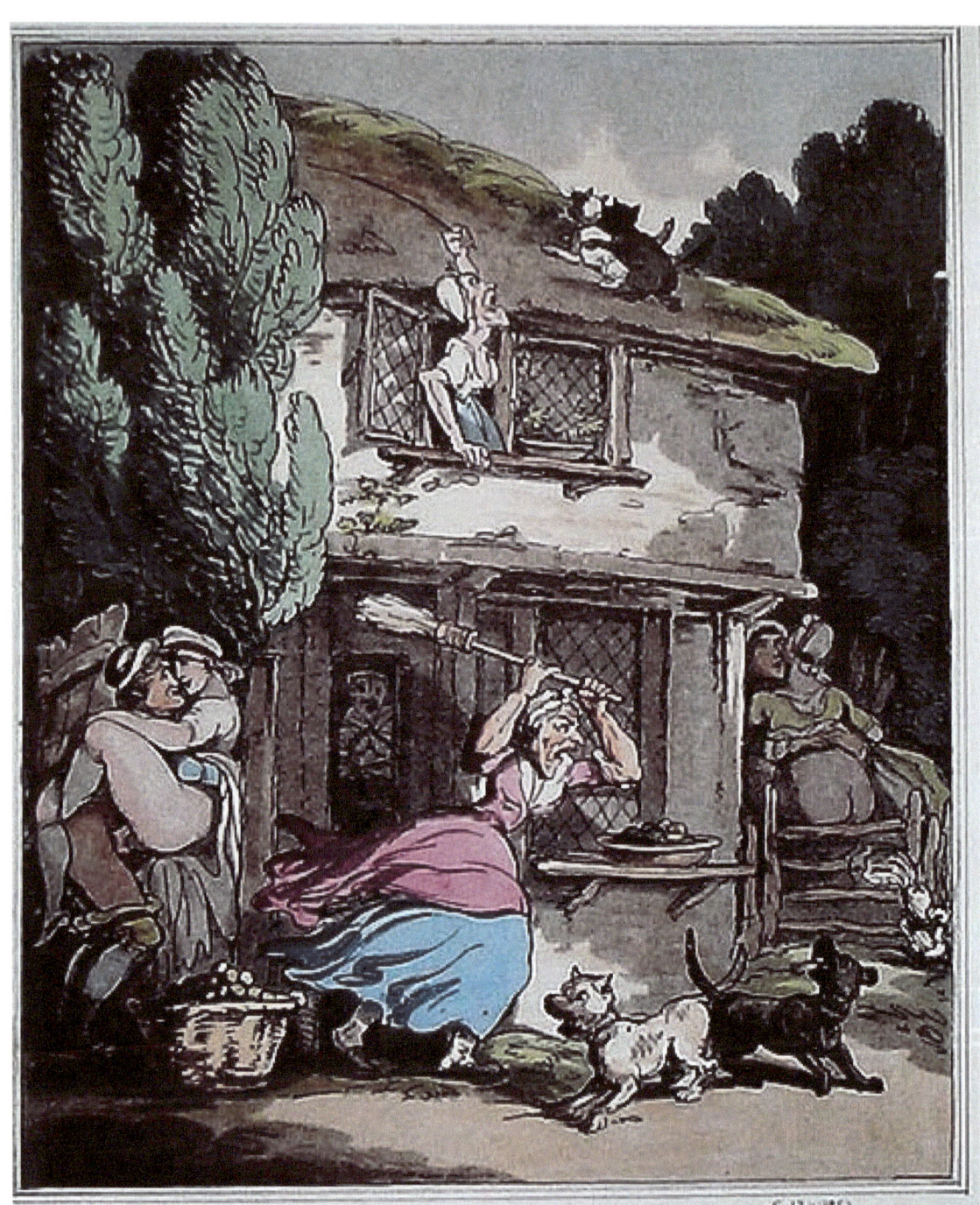

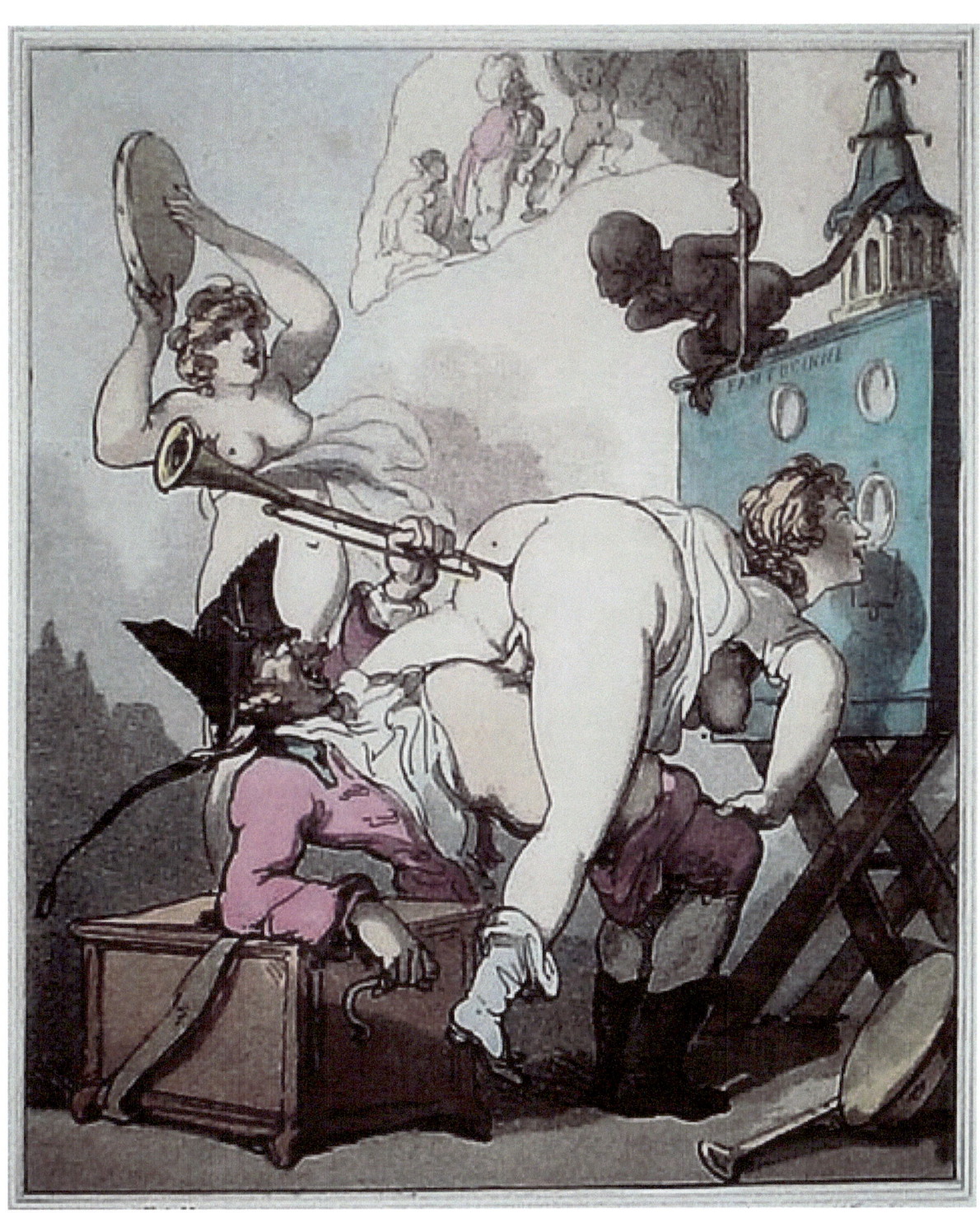

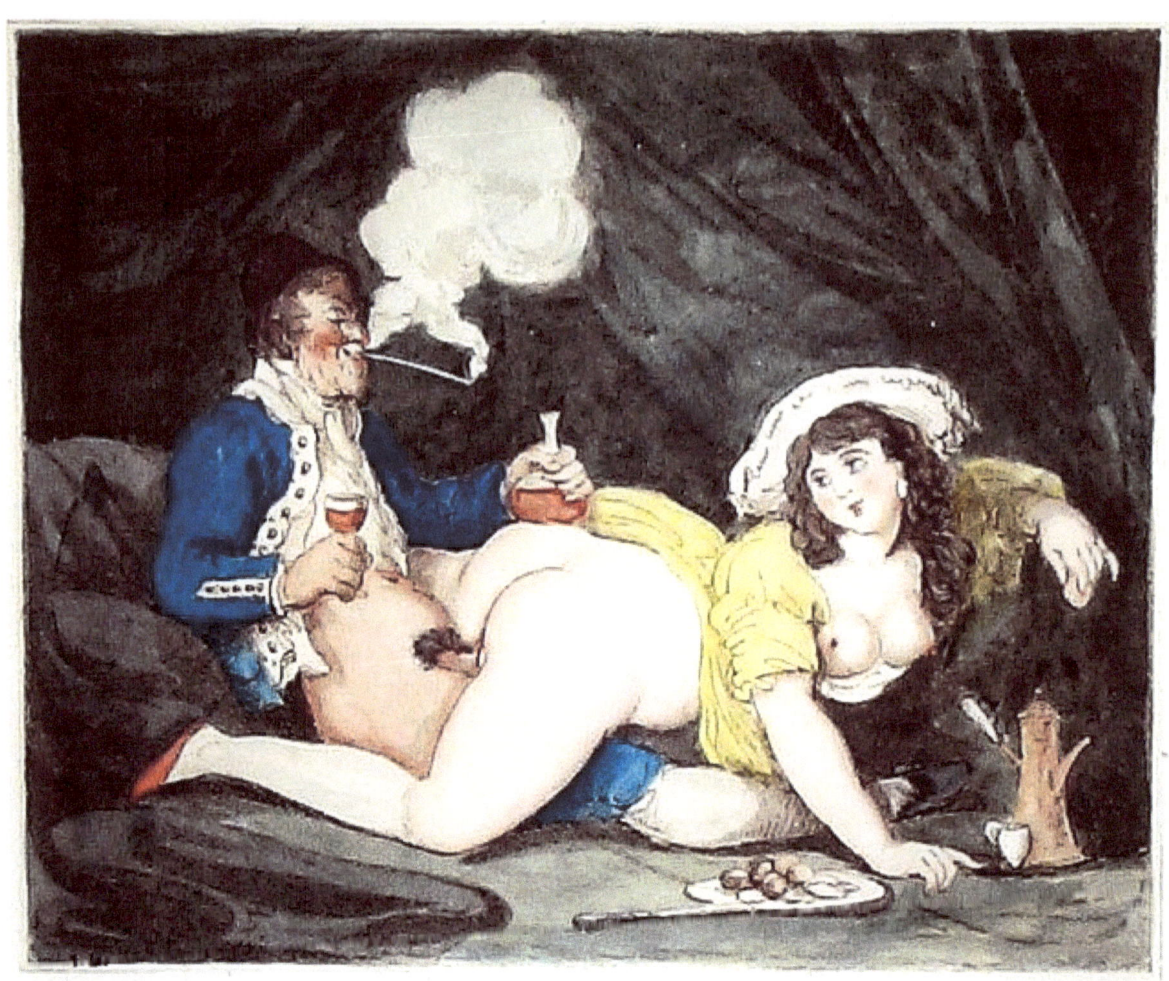

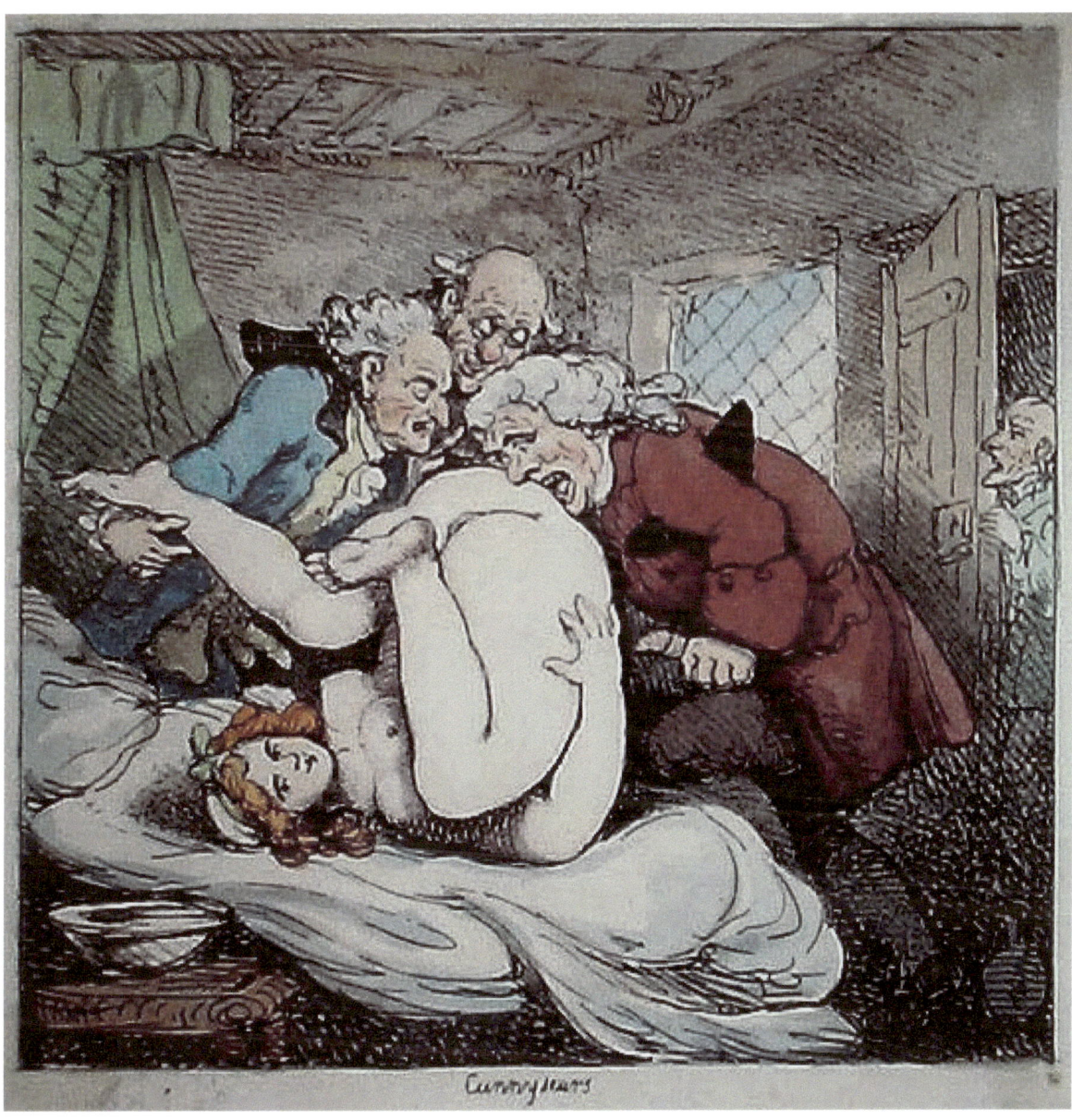

Cunning dreams

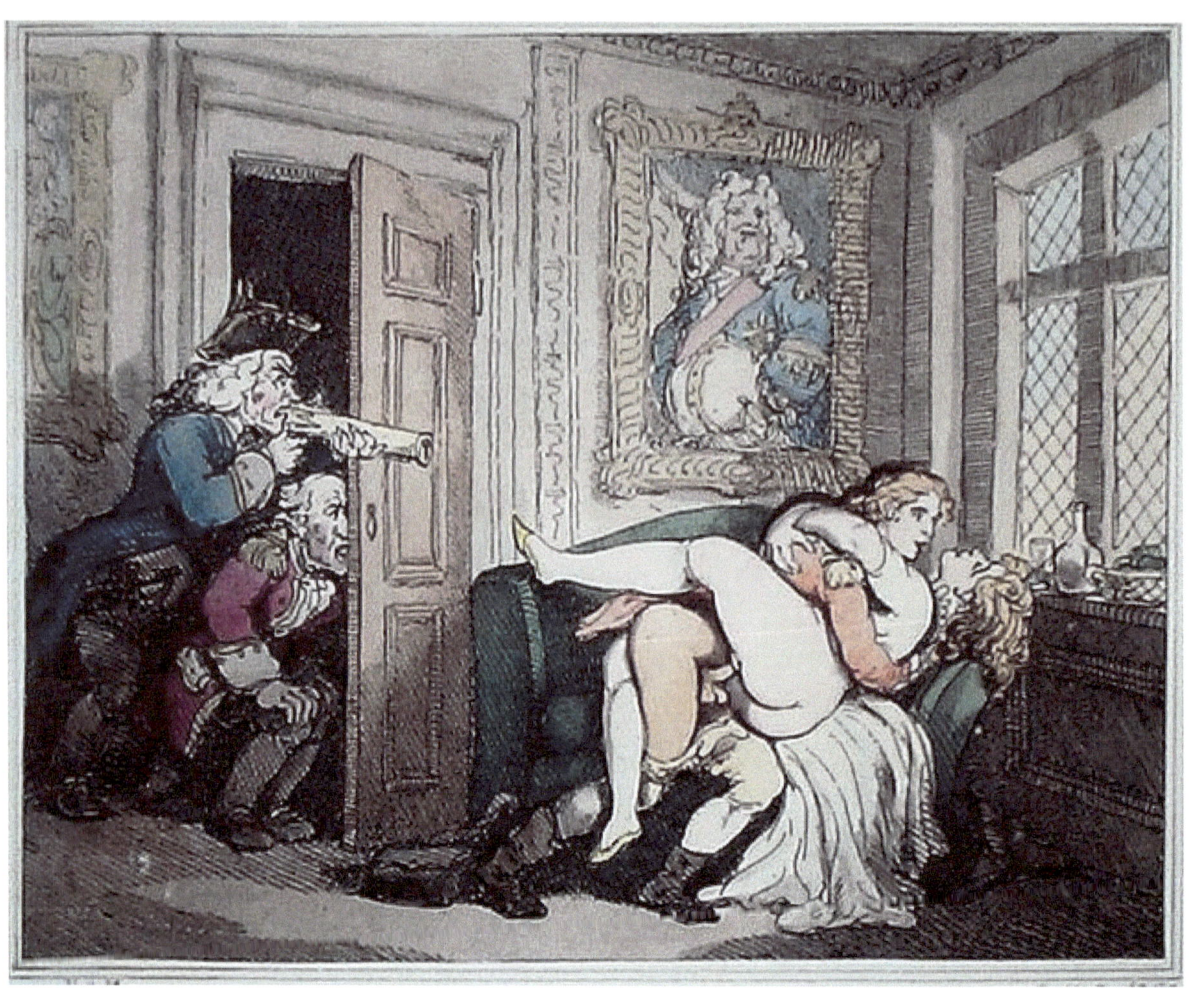

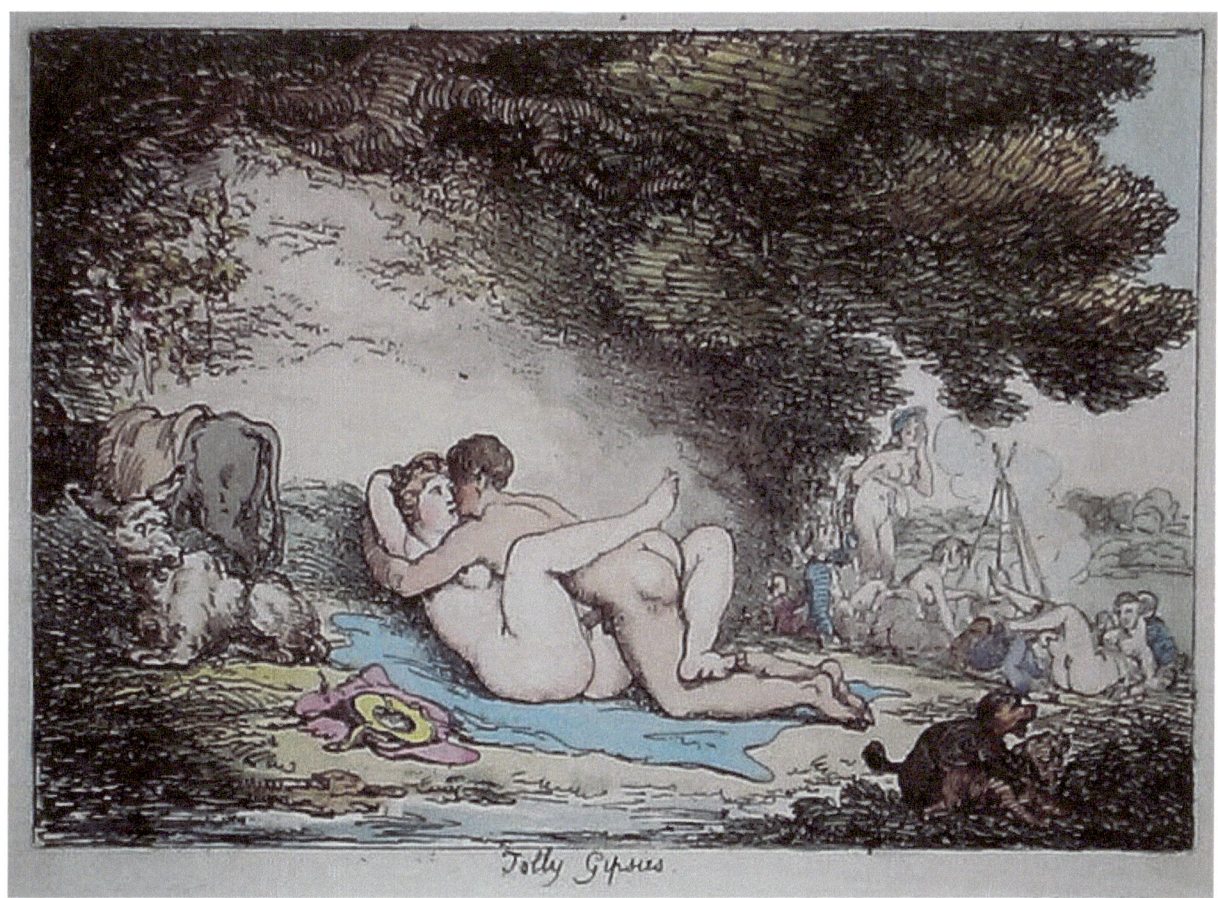

Jolly Gipsies

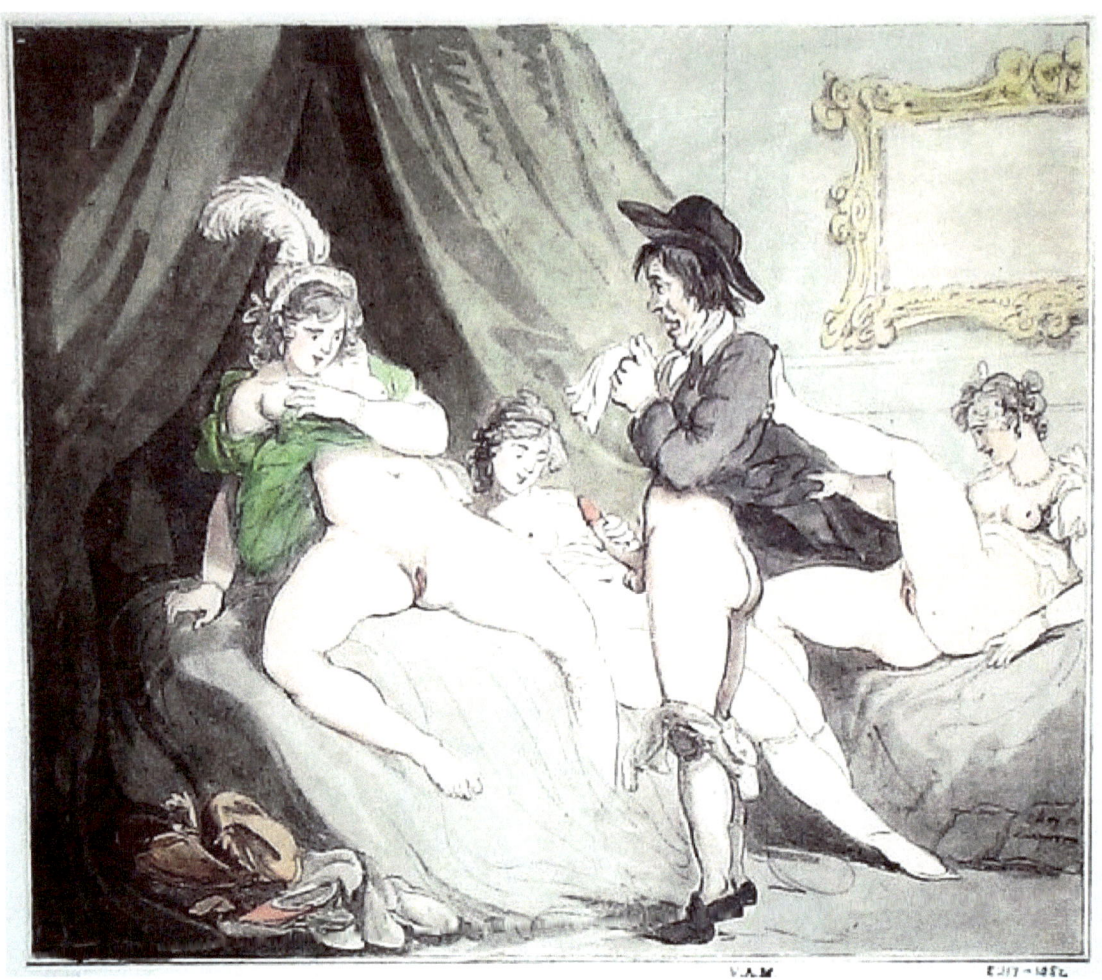

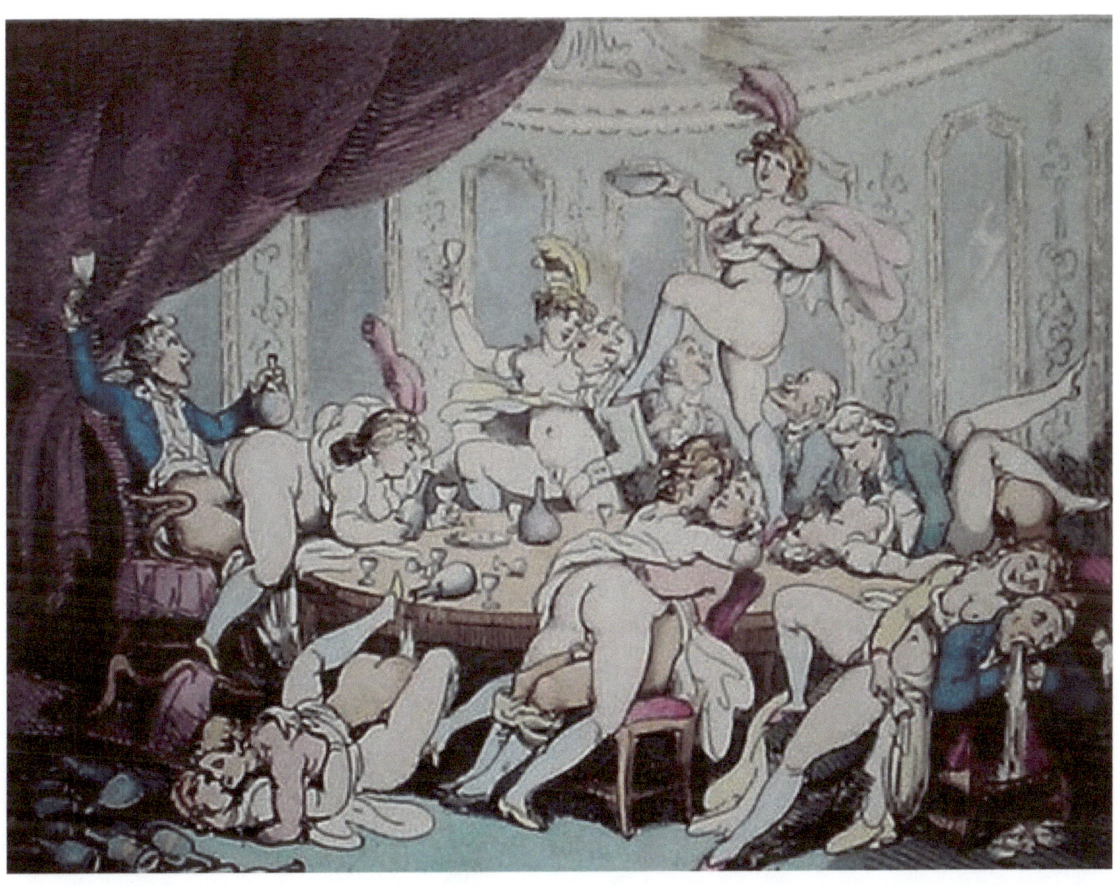

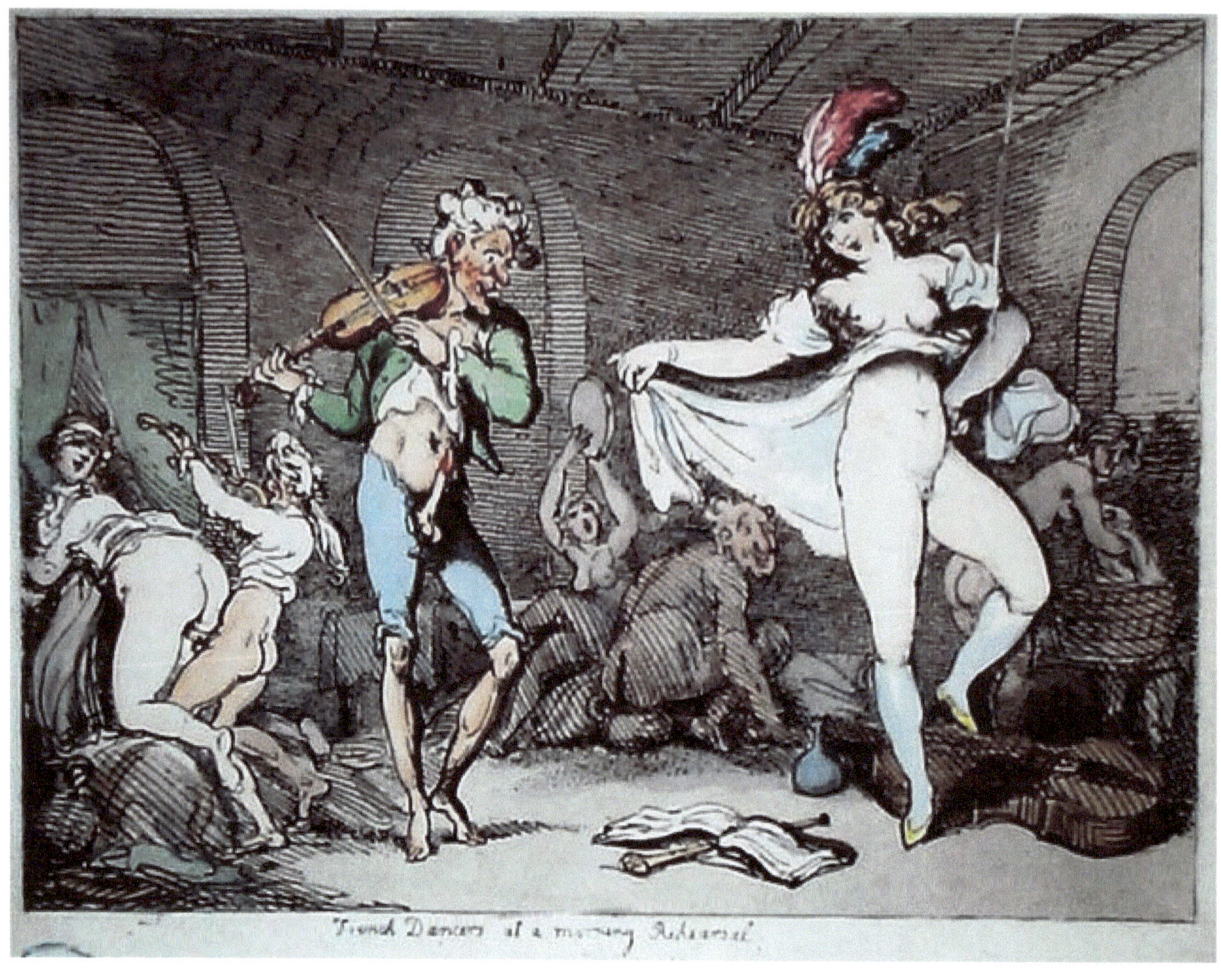

French Dancers at a morning Rehearsal

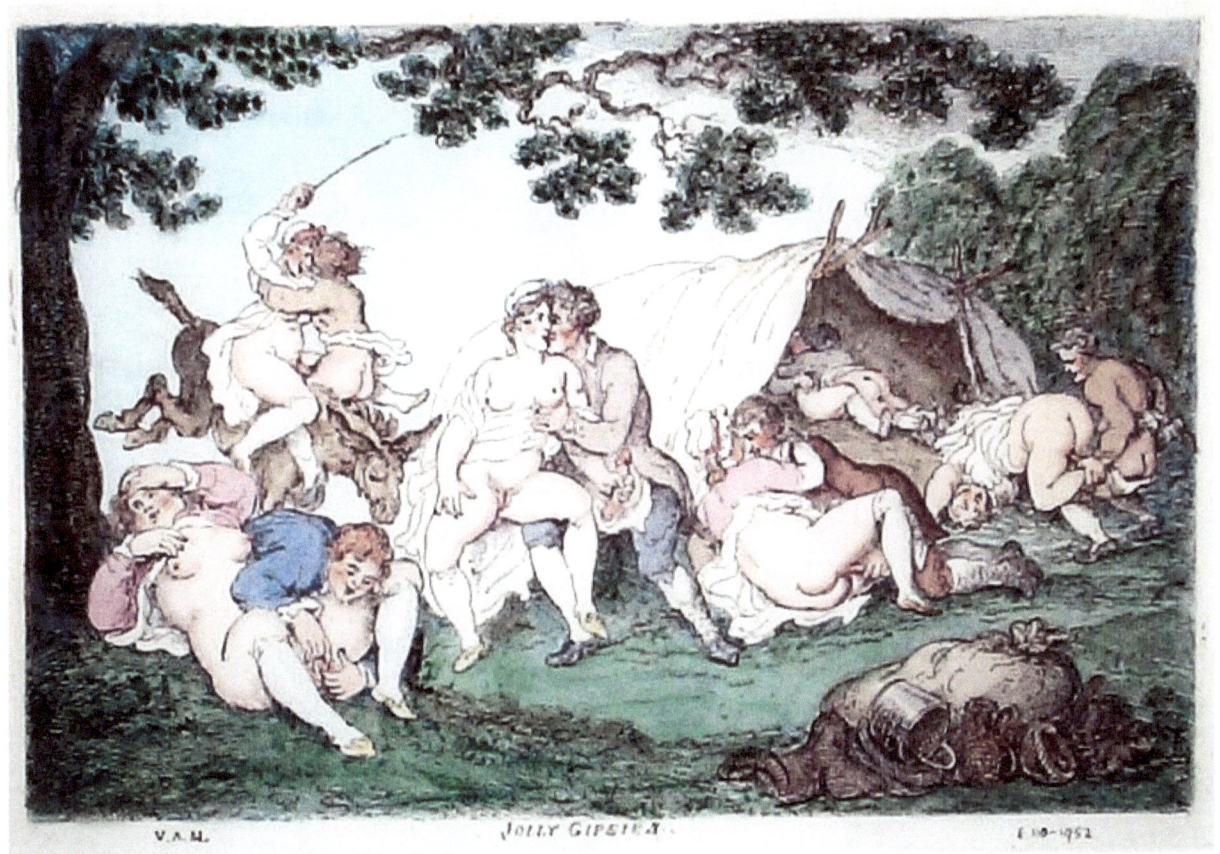

Jolly Gipsies

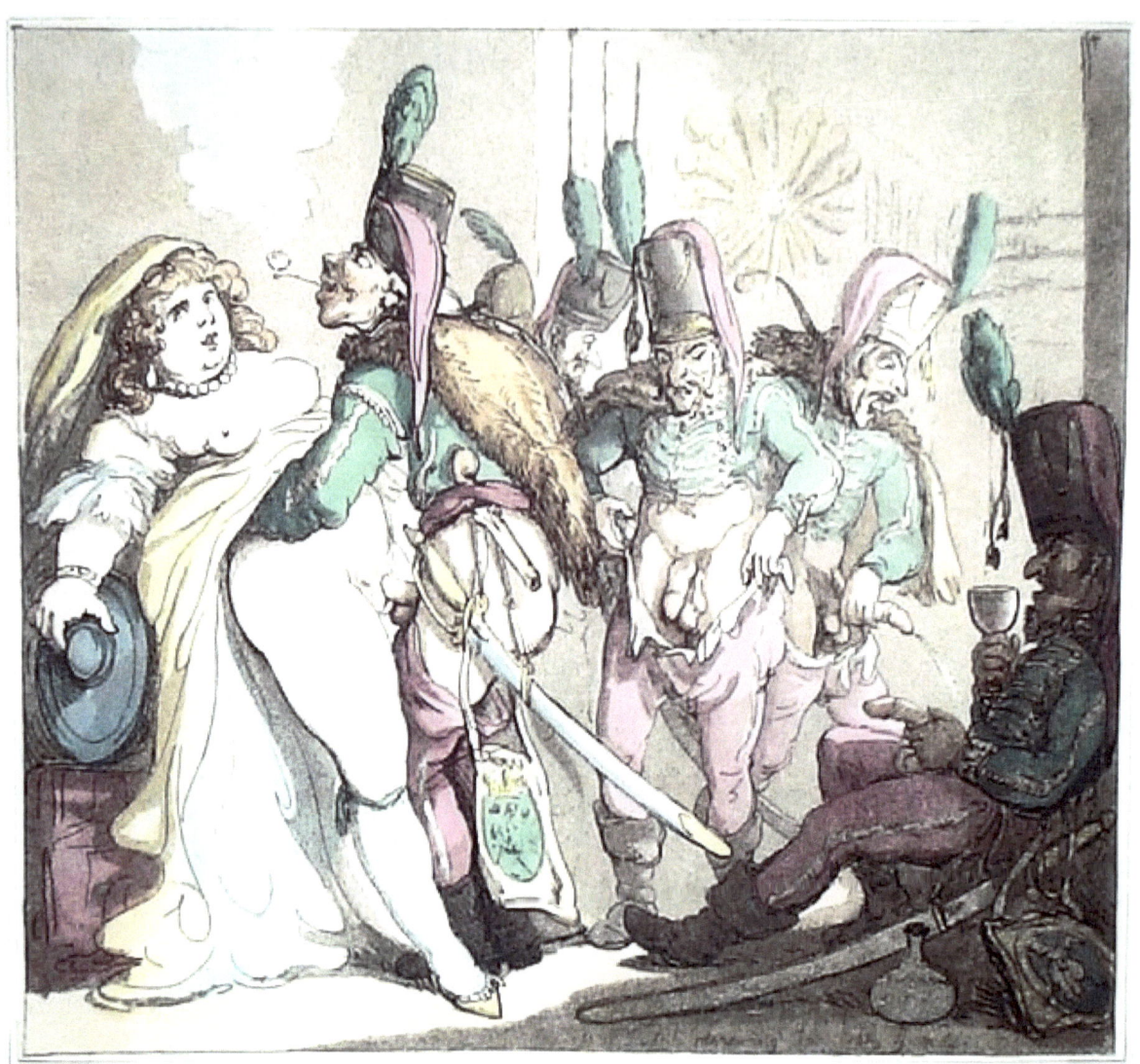

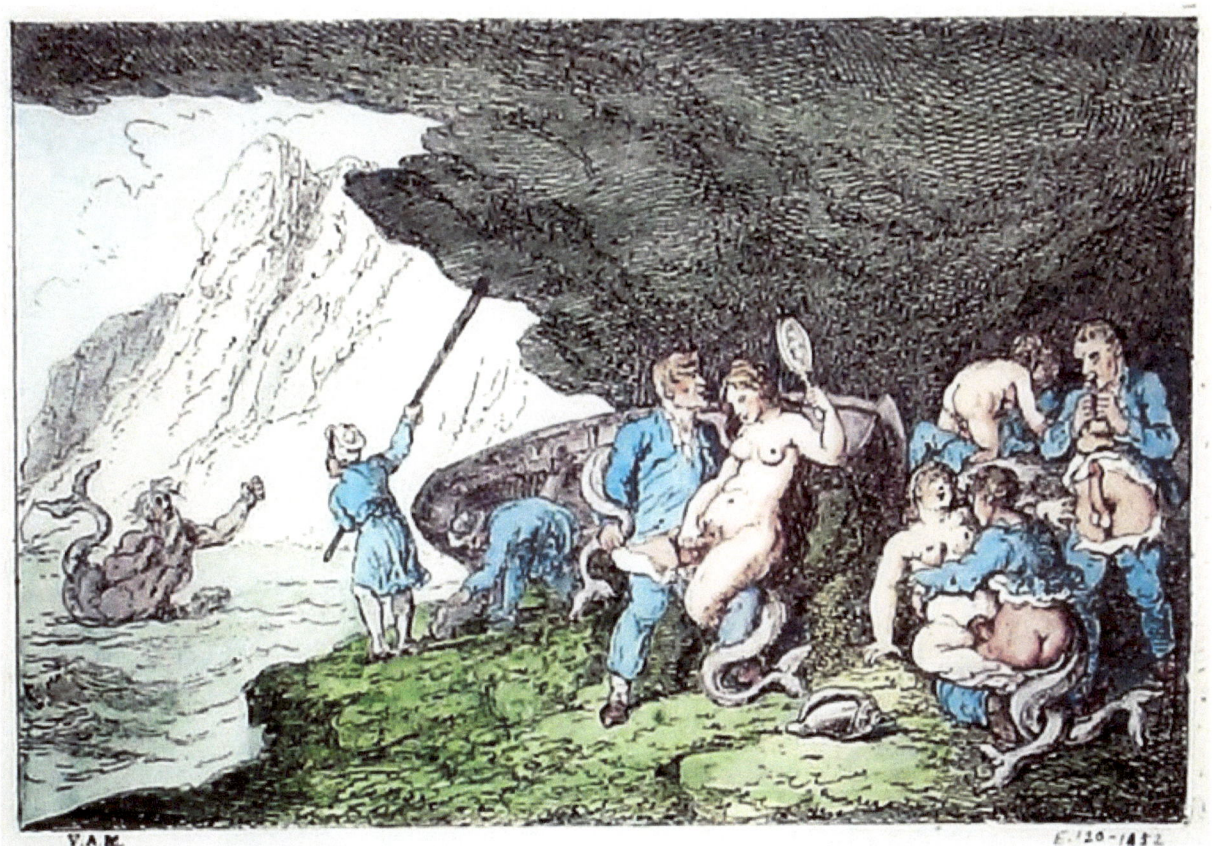

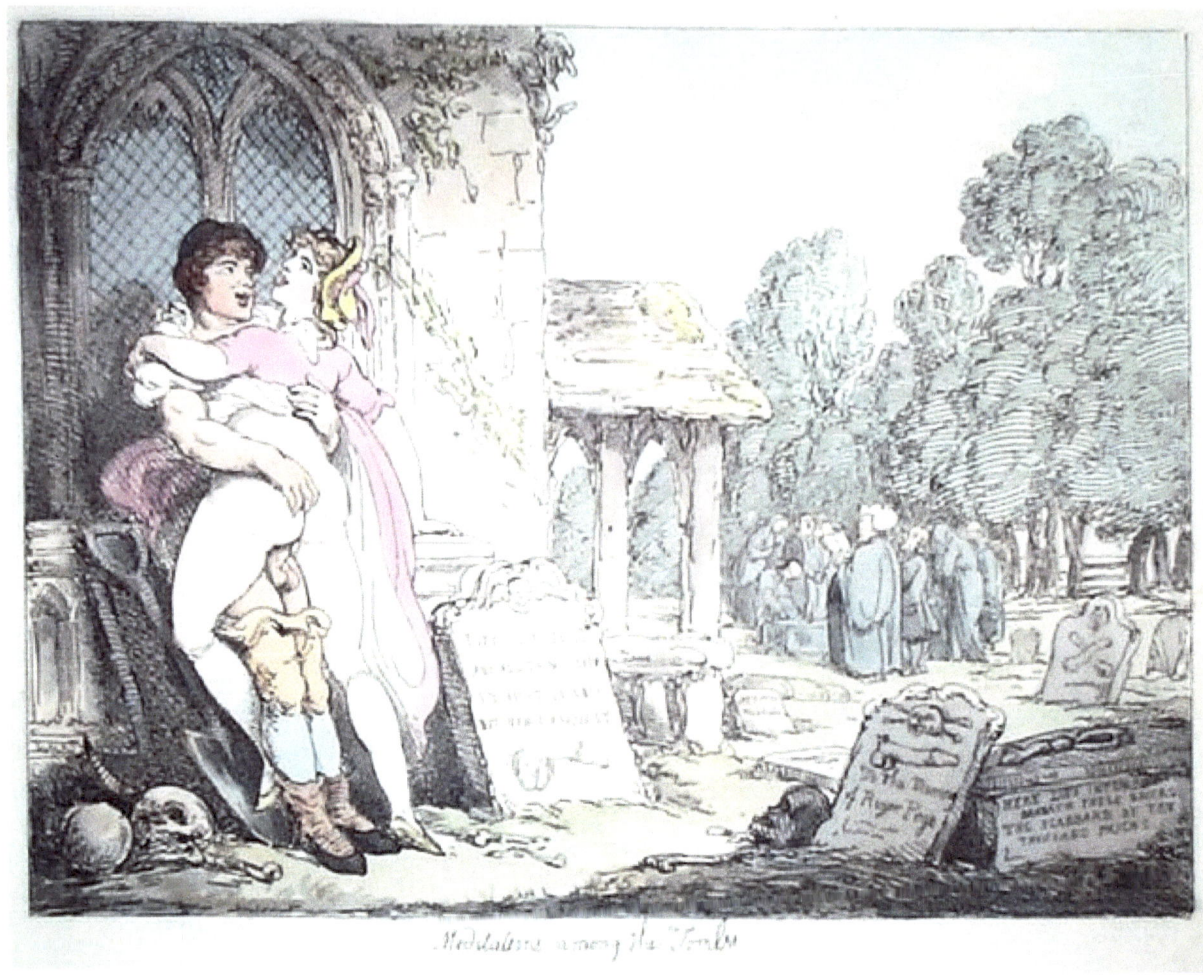

Meditation among the Tombs